Mometrix
TEST PREPARATION

MCA

Success Strategies
Grade 8
Reading

I0889138

DEAR FUTURE EXAM SUCCESS STORY

First of all, **THANK YOU** for purchasing Mometrix study materials!

Second, congratulations! You are one of the few determined test-takers who are committed to doing whatever it takes to excel on your exam. **You have come to the right place.** We developed these study materials with one goal in mind: to deliver you the information you need in a format that's concise and easy to use.

In addition to optimizing your guide for the content of the test, we've outlined our recommended steps for breaking down the preparation process into small, attainable goals so you can make sure you stay on track.

We've also analyzed the entire test-taking process, identifying the most common pitfalls and showing how you can overcome them and be ready for any curveball the test throws you.

Standardized testing is one of the biggest obstacles on your road to success, which only increases the importance of doing well in the high-pressure, high-stakes environment of test day. Your results on this test could have a significant impact on your future, and this guide provides the information and practical advice to help you achieve your full potential on test day.

Your success is our success

We would love to hear from you! If you would like to share the story of your exam success or if you have any questions or comments in regard to our products, please contact us at **800-673-8175** or **support@mometrix.com**.

Thanks again for your business and we wish you continued success!

Sincerely,
The Mometrix Test Preparation Team

Written and edited by the Mometrix Test Preparation Team
Printed in the United States of America

TABLE OF CONTENTS

Introduction

Thank you for purchasing this resource! You have made the choice to prepare yourself for a test that could have a huge impact on your future, and this guide is designed to help you be fully ready for test day. Obviously, it's important to have a solid understanding of the test material, but you also need to be prepared for the unique environment and stressors of the test, so that you can perform to the best of your abilities.

For this purpose, the first section that appears in this guide is the **Success Strategies**. We've devoted countless hours to meticulously researching what works and what doesn't, and we've boiled down our findings to the most impactful steps you can take to improve your performance on the test. We start at the beginning with study planning and move through the preparation process, all the way to the testing strategies that will help you get the most out of what you know when you're finally sitting in front of the test.

We recommend that you start preparing for your test as far in advance as possible. However, if you've bought this guide as a last-minute study resource and only have a few days before your test, we recommend that you skip over the first two Success Strategies since they address a long-term study plan.

If you struggle with **test anxiety**, we strongly encourage you to check out our recommendations for how you can overcome it. Test anxiety is a formidable foe, but it can be beaten, and we want to make sure you have the tools you need to defeat it.

Strategy #1 – Plan Big, Study Small

There's a lot riding on your performance. If you want to ace this test, you're going to need to keep your skills sharp and the material fresh in your mind. You need a plan that lets you review everything you need to know while still fitting in your schedule. We'll break this strategy down into three categories.

Information Organization

Start with the information you already have: the official test outline. From this, you can make a complete list of all the concepts you need to cover before the test. Organize these concepts into groups that can be studied together, and create a list of any related vocabulary you need to learn so you can brush up on any difficult terms. You'll want to keep this vocabulary list handy once you actually start studying since you may need to add to it along the way.

Time Management

Once you have your set of study concepts, decide how to spread them out over the time you have left before the test. Break your study plan into small, clear goals so you have a manageable task for each day and know exactly what you're doing. Then just focus on one small step at a time. When you manage your time this way, you don't need to spend hours at a time studying. Studying a small block of content for a short period each day helps you retain information better and avoid stressing over how much you have left to do. You can relax knowing that you have a plan to cover everything in time. In order for this strategy to be effective though, you have to start studying early and stick to your schedule. Avoid the exhaustion and futility that comes from last-minute cramming!

Study Environment

The environment you study in has a big impact on your learning. Studying in a coffee shop, while probably more enjoyable, is not likely to be as fruitful as studying in a quiet room. It's important to keep distractions to a minimum. You're only planning to study for a short block of time, so make the most of it. Don't pause to check your phone or get up to find a snack. It's also important to **avoid multitasking**. Research has consistently shown that multitasking will make your studying dramatically less effective. Your study area should also be comfortable and well-lit so you don't have the distraction of straining your eyes or sitting on an uncomfortable chair.

The time of day you study is also important. You want to be rested and alert. Don't wait until just before bedtime. Study when you'll be most likely to comprehend and remember. Even better, if you know what time of day your test will be, set that time aside for study. That way your brain will be used to working on that subject at that specific time and you'll have a better chance of recalling information.

Finally, it can be helpful to team up with others who are studying for the same test. Your actual studying should be done in as isolated an environment as possible, but the work of organizing the information and setting up the study plan can be divided up. In between study sessions, you can discuss with your teammates the concepts that you're all studying and quiz each other on the details. Just be sure that your teammates are as serious about the test as you are. If you find that your study time is being replaced with social time, you might need to find a new team.

Strategy #2 – Make Your Studying Count

You're devoting a lot of time and effort to preparing for this test, so you want to be absolutely certain it will pay off. This means doing more than just reading the content and hoping you can remember it on test day. It's important to make every minute of study count. There are two main areas you can focus on to make your studying count.

Retention

It doesn't matter how much time you study if you can't remember the material. You need to make sure you are retaining the concepts. To check your retention of the information you're learning, try recalling it at later times with minimal prompting. Try carrying around flashcards and glance at one or two from time to time or ask a friend who's also studying for the test to quiz you.

To enhance your retention, look for ways to put the information into practice so that you can apply it rather than simply recalling it. If you're using the information in practical ways, it will be much easier to remember. Similarly, it helps to solidify a concept in your mind if you're not only reading it to yourself but also explaining it to someone else. Ask a friend to let you teach them about a concept you're a little shaky on (or speak aloud to an imaginary audience if necessary). As you try to summarize, define, give examples, and answer your friend's questions, you'll understand the concepts better and they will stay with you longer. Finally, step back for a big picture view and ask yourself how each piece of information fits with the whole subject. When you link the different concepts together and see them working together as a whole, it's easier to remember the individual components.

Finally, practice showing your work on any multi-step problems, even if you're just studying. Writing out each step you take to solve a problem will help solidify the process in your mind, and you'll be more likely to remember it during the test.

Modality

Modality simply refers to the means or method by which you study. Choosing a study modality that fits your own individual learning style is crucial. No two people learn best in exactly the same way, so it's important to know your strengths and use them to your advantage.

For example, if you learn best by visualization, focus on visualizing a concept in your mind and draw an image or a diagram. Try color-coding your notes, illustrating them, or creating symbols that will trigger your mind to recall a learned concept. If you learn best by hearing or discussing information, find a study partner who learns the same way or read aloud to yourself. Think about how to put the information in your own words. Imagine that you are giving a lecture on the topic and record yourself so you can listen to it later.

For any learning style, flashcards can be helpful. Organize the information so you can take advantage of spare moments to review. Underline key words or phrases. Use different colors for different categories. Mnemonic devices (such as creating a short list in which every item starts with the same letter) can also help with retention. Find what works best for you and use it to store the information in your mind most effectively and easily.

Strategy #3 – Practice the Right Way

Your success on test day depends not only on how many hours you put into preparing, but also on whether you prepared the right way. It's good to check along the way to see if your studying is paying off. One of the most effective ways to do this is by taking practice tests to evaluate your progress. Practice tests are useful because they show exactly where you need to improve. Every time you take a practice test, pay special attention to these three groups of questions:

- The questions you got wrong
- The questions you had to guess on, even if you guessed right
- The questions you found difficult or slow to work through

This will show you exactly what your weak areas are, and where you need to devote more study time. Ask yourself why each of these questions gave you trouble. Was it because you didn't understand the material? Was it because you didn't remember the vocabulary? Do you need more repetitions on this type of question to build speed and confidence? Dig into those questions and figure out how you can strengthen your weak areas as you go back to review the material.

Additionally, many practice tests have a section explaining the answer choices. It can be tempting to read the explanation and think that you now have a good understanding of the concept. However, an explanation likely only covers part of the question's broader context. Even if the explanation makes perfect sense, **go back and investigate** every concept related to the question until you're positive you have a thorough understanding.

As you go along, keep in mind that the practice test is just that: practice. Memorizing these questions and answers will not be very helpful on the actual test because it is unlikely to have any of the same exact questions. If you only know the right answers to the sample questions, you won't be prepared for the real thing. **Study the concepts** until you understand them fully, and then you'll be able to answer any question that shows up on the test.

It's important to wait on the practice tests until you're ready. If you take a test on your first day of study, you may be overwhelmed by the amount of material covered and how much you need to learn. Work up to it gradually.

On test day, you'll need to be prepared for answering questions, managing your time, and using the test-taking strategies you've learned. It's a lot to balance, like a mental marathon that will have a big impact on your future. Like training for a marathon, you'll need to start slowly and work your way up. When test day arrives, you'll be ready.

Start with the strategies you've read in the first two Success Strategies—plan your course and study in the way that works best for you. If you have time, consider using multiple study resources to get different approaches to the same concepts. It can be helpful to see difficult concepts from more than one angle. Then find a good source for practice tests. Many times, the test website will suggest potential study resources or provide sample tests.

Practice Test Strategy

If you're able to find at least three practice tests, we recommend this strategy:

Untimed and Open-Book Practice

Take the first test with no time constraints and with your notes and study guide handy. Take your time and focus on applying the strategies you've learned.

Timed and Open-Book Practice

Take the second practice test open-book as well, but set a timer and practice pacing yourself to finish in time.

Timed and Closed-Book Practice

Take any other practice tests as if it were test day. Set a timer and put away your study materials. Sit at a table or desk in a quiet room, imagine yourself at the testing center, and answer questions as quickly and accurately as possible.

Keep repeating timed and closed-book tests on a regular basis until you run out of practice tests or it's time for the actual test. Your mind will be ready for the schedule and stress of test day, and you'll be able to focus on recalling the material you've learned.

Strategy #4 – Pace Yourself

Once you're fully prepared for the material on the test, your biggest challenge on test day will be managing your time. Just knowing that the clock is ticking can make you panic even if you have plenty of time left. Work on pacing yourself so you can build confidence against the time constraints of the exam. Pacing is a difficult skill to master, especially in a high-pressure environment, so **practice is vital**.

Set time expectations for your pace based on how much time is available. For example, if a section has 60 questions and the time limit is 30 minutes, you know you have to average 30 seconds or less per question in order to answer them all. Although 30 seconds is the hard limit, set 25 seconds per question as your goal, so you reserve extra time to spend on harder questions. When you budget extra time for the harder questions, you no longer have any reason to stress when those questions take longer to answer.

Don't let this time expectation distract you from working through the test at a calm, steady pace, but keep it in mind so you don't spend too much time on any one question. Recognize that taking extra time on one question you don't understand may keep you from answering two that you do understand later in the test. If your time limit for a question is up and you're still not sure of the answer, mark it and move on, and come back to it later if the time and the test format allow. If the testing format doesn't allow you to return to earlier questions, just make an educated guess; then put it out of your mind and move on.

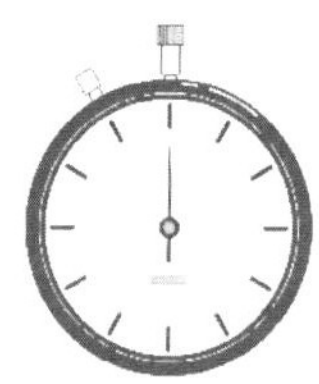

On the easier questions, be careful not to rush. It may seem wise to hurry through them so you have more time for the challenging ones, but it's not worth missing one if you know the concept and just didn't take the time to read the question fully. Work efficiently but make sure you understand the question and have looked at all of the answer choices, since more than one may seem right at first.

Even if you're paying attention to the time, you may find yourself a little behind at some point. You should speed up to get back on track, but do so wisely. Don't panic; just take a few seconds less on each question until you're caught up. Don't guess without thinking, but do look through the answer choices and eliminate any you know are wrong. If you can get down to two choices, it is often worthwhile to guess from those. Once you've chosen an answer, move on and don't dwell on any that you skipped or had to hurry through. If a question was taking too long, chances are it was one of the harder ones, so you weren't as likely to get it right anyway.

On the other hand, if you find yourself getting ahead of schedule, it may be beneficial to slow down a little. The more quickly you work, the more likely you are to make a careless mistake that will affect your score. You've budgeted time for each question, so don't be afraid to spend that time. Practice an efficient but careful pace to get the most out of the time you have.

Test-Taking Strategies

This section contains a list of test-taking strategies that you may find helpful as you work through the test. By taking what you know and applying logical thought, you can maximize your chances of answering any question correctly!

It is very important to realize that every question is different and every person is different: no single strategy will work on every question, and no single strategy will work for every person. That's why we've included all of them here, so you can try them out and determine which ones work best for different types of questions and which ones work best for you.

Question Strategies

⊘ Read Carefully

Read the question and the answer choices carefully. Don't miss the question because you misread the terms. You have plenty of time to read each question thoroughly and make sure you understand what is being asked. Yet a happy medium must be attained, so don't waste too much time. You must read carefully and efficiently.

⊘ Contextual Clues

Look for contextual clues. If the question includes a word you are not familiar with, look at the immediate context for some indication of what the word might mean. Contextual clues can often give you all the information you need to decipher the meaning of an unfamiliar word. Even if you can't determine the meaning, you may be able to narrow down the possibilities enough to make a solid guess at the answer to the question.

⊘ Prefixes

If you're having trouble with a word in the question or answer choices, try dissecting it. Take advantage of every clue that the word might include. Prefixes can be a huge help. Usually, they allow you to determine a basic meaning. *Pre-* means before, *post-* means after, *pro-* is positive, *de-* is negative. From prefixes, you can get an idea of the general meaning of the word and try to put it into context.

⊘ Hedge Words

Watch out for critical hedge words, such as *likely, may, can, often, almost, mostly, usually, generally, rarely*, and *sometimes*. Question writers insert these hedge phrases to cover every possibility. Often an answer choice will be wrong simply because it leaves no room for exception. Be on guard for answer choices that have definitive words such as *exactly* and *always*.

⊘ Switchback Words

Stay alert for *switchbacks*. These are the words and phrases frequently used to alert you to shifts in thought. The most common switchback words are *but, although*, and *however*. Others include *nevertheless, on the other hand, even though, while, in spite of, despite*, and *regardless of*. Switchback words are important to catch because they can change the direction of the question or an answer choice.

✓ Face Value

When in doubt, use common sense. Accept the situation in the problem at face value. Don't read too much into it. These problems will not require you to make wild assumptions. If you have to go beyond creativity and warp time or space in order to have an answer choice fit the question, then you should move on and consider the other answer choices. These are normal problems rooted in reality. The applicable relationship or explanation may not be readily apparent, but it is there for you to figure out. Use your common sense to interpret anything that isn't clear.

Answer Choice Strategies

✓ Answer Selection

The most thorough way to pick an answer choice is to identify and eliminate wrong answers until only one is left, then confirm it is the correct answer. Sometimes an answer choice may immediately seem right, but be careful. The test writers will usually put more than one reasonable answer choice on each question, so take a second to read all of them and make sure that the other choices are not equally obvious. As long as you have time left, it is better to read every answer choice than to pick the first one that looks right without checking the others.

✓ Answer Choice Families

An answer choice family consists of two (in rare cases, three) answer choices that are very similar in construction and cannot all be true at the same time. If you see two answer choices that are direct opposites or parallels, one of them is usually the correct answer. For instance, if one answer choice says that quantity *x* increases and another either says that quantity *x* decreases (opposite) or says that quantity *y* increases (parallel), then those answer choices would fall into the same family. An answer choice that doesn't match the construction of the answer choice family is more likely to be incorrect. Most questions will not have answer choice families, but when they do appear, you should be prepared to recognize them.

✓ Eliminate Answers

Eliminate answer choices as soon as you realize they are wrong, but make sure you consider all possibilities. If you are eliminating answer choices and realize that the last one you are left with is also wrong, don't panic. Start over and consider each choice again. There may be something you missed the first time that you will realize on the second pass.

✓ Avoid Fact Traps

Don't be distracted by an answer choice that is factually true but doesn't answer the question. You are looking for the choice that answers the question. Stay focused on what the question is asking for so you don't accidentally pick an answer that is true but incorrect. Always go back to the question and make sure the answer choice you've selected actually answers the question and is not merely a true statement.

✓ Extreme Statements

In general, you should avoid answers that put forth extreme actions as standard practice or proclaim controversial ideas as established fact. An answer choice that states the "process should be used in certain situations, if..." is much more likely to be correct than one that states the "process should be discontinued completely." The first is a calm rational statement and doesn't even make a definitive, uncompromising stance, using a hedge word *if* to provide wiggle room, whereas the second choice is far more extreme.

⊘ Benchmark

As you read through the answer choices and you come across one that seems to answer the question well, mentally select that answer choice. This is not your final answer, but it's the one that will help you evaluate the other answer choices. The one that you selected is your benchmark or standard for judging each of the other answer choices. Every other answer choice must be compared to your benchmark. That choice is correct until proven otherwise by another answer choice beating it. If you find a better answer, then that one becomes your new benchmark. Once you've decided that no other choice answers the question as well as your benchmark, you have your final answer.

⊘ Predict the Answer

Before you even start looking at the answer choices, it is often best to try to predict the answer. When you come up with the answer on your own, it is easier to avoid distractions and traps because you will know exactly what to look for. The right answer choice is unlikely to be word-for-word what you came up with, but it should be a close match. Even if you are confident that you have the right answer, you should still take the time to read each option before moving on.

General Strategies

⊘ Tough Questions

If you are stumped on a problem or it appears too hard or too difficult, don't waste time. Move on! Remember though, if you can quickly check for obviously incorrect answer choices, your chances of guessing correctly are greatly improved. Before you completely give up, at least try to knock out a couple of possible answers. Eliminate what you can and then guess at the remaining answer choices before moving on.

⊘ Check Your Work

Since you will probably not know every term listed and the answer to every question, it is important that you get credit for the ones that you do know. Don't miss any questions through careless mistakes. If at all possible, try to take a second to look back over your answer selection and make sure you've selected the correct answer choice and haven't made a costly careless mistake (such as marking an answer choice that you didn't mean to mark). This quick double check should more than pay for itself in caught mistakes for the time it costs.

⊘ Pace Yourself

It's easy to be overwhelmed when you're looking at a page full of questions; your mind is confused and full of random thoughts, and the clock is ticking down faster than you would like. Calm down and maintain the pace that you have set for yourself. Especially as you get down to the last few minutes of the test, don't let the small numbers on the clock make you panic. As long as you are on track by monitoring your pace, you are guaranteed to have time for each question.

⊘ Don't Rush

It is very easy to make errors when you are in a hurry. Maintaining a fast pace in answering questions is pointless if it makes you miss questions that you would have gotten right otherwise. Test writers like to include distracting information and wrong answers that seem right. Taking a little extra time to avoid careless mistakes can make all the difference in your test score. Find a pace that allows you to be confident in the answers that you select.

☑ KEEP MOVING

Panicking will not help you pass the test, so do your best to stay calm and keep moving. Taking deep breaths and going through the answer elimination steps you practiced can help to break through a stress barrier and keep your pace.

Final Notes

The combination of a solid foundation of content knowledge and the confidence that comes from practicing your plan for applying that knowledge is the key to maximizing your performance on test day. As your foundation of content knowledge is built up and strengthened, you'll find that the strategies included in this chapter become more and more effective in helping you quickly sift through the distractions and traps of the test to isolate the correct answer.

Now that you're preparing to move forward into the test content chapters of this book, be sure to keep your goal in mind. As you read, think about how you will be able to apply this information on the test. If you've already seen sample questions for the test and you have an idea of the question format and style, try to come up with questions of your own that you can answer based on what you're reading. This will give you valuable practice applying your knowledge in the same ways you can expect to on test day.

Good luck and good studying!

Reading

Using Print and Digital Resources

Dictionary

A print or digital dictionary can be used to find out many things about a word. A dictionary will show the correct pronunciation of a word, provide its meaning, and identify what part of speech the word is. It will also tell how the word was derived—that is, what words it came from originally. A dictionary will have a guide that shows how to sound out the words; it will use symbols to indicate sounds, and will also use sample sounds (the "a" in "bad," for instance). A dictionary lists all of the meanings of a word and the parts of speech the word can be used as.

Example

Philippe used his dictionary to check the various meanings of the word *eliminate*. He found this entry:

> eliminate \ i-'li-mə-ˌnāt \ verb
> 1. to put an end to or get rid of
> 2. to expel from the living body
> 3. to cause to disappear by combining two or more equations

Identify which definition of *eliminate* is used in the following sentence:

> Harold couldn't wait to *eliminate* the other team from the playoffs by winning the first two games.

The correct answer is meaning 1: "to put an end to or get rid of." If you substitute that definition for the word, the sentence makes sense. Meanings 2 and 3 do not fit with the context of the sentence. When considering which meaning is being used, always check for context clues in the sentence or in the sentences before or after the sentence in which the word is used. Dictionaries also tell you how to pronounce words and often the derivation of the word, although that is not given here.

Thesaurus

A thesaurus is a reference book that gives synonyms of words. It is different from a dictionary because a thesaurus does not give definitions. A thesaurus can be helpful in finding the meaning of an unfamiliar word when reading. If the meaning of a synonym is known, then the meaning of the unfamiliar word will be known. Another time in which a thesaurus can be helpful is when writing. Using a thesaurus helps authors to vary their word choice.

Glossary

A glossary is a list of terms and their definitions that can be found at the back of certain types of books, such as textbooks or reference books. A glossary does not have the definitions of all words, like a dictionary, but instead gives the definitions of the important terms within that particular book which are either uncommon or newly introduced. One may use a glossary when reading a book about economics or a chapter in a science textbook, for example, to define some of the technical terms within the text.

Denotative and Connotative Meaning

The **denotative meaning** of a word is the exact dictionary definition of the word. The **connotative meaning** of a word is the emotion conveyed by the use of the word in context. The word may have associated meaning in addition to its dictionary definition. A good way to remember the difference between denotative and connotative is to think "direct" or "dictionary" in relation to denotative.

An example of a denotative meaning for the adjective *ablaze* would be "burning", as in the logs burning in a fireplace. A connotative meaning for the adjective *ablaze*, based on the context of the word, may indicate a level of comfort while sitting in front of a fireplace. For instance, in the context: "A logs were *ablaze* in the fireplace, radiating heat out into the corners of the snow-enclosed room", the word *ablaze* implies comfort and coziness within the space described. The connotative meaning of a word can often have an emotional association for the reader.

Example

Define the denotative and connotative meaning of the word *palace* in the following sentence:

> The golden *palace* gates opened slowly to reveal an expansive garden that was well-tended by precise gardeners all wearing the king's insignia.

In the example, the denotative meaning of the word is that a *palace* is literally a place where royalty lives. A *palace* implies, or connotes, a place of riches and is usually associated with wealth. The words "golden", "expansive garden", and "king's insignia" all give clues that the *palace* can be viewed as a place of importance, one that is well taken care of.

When looking for the denotative meaning of a word, remember to think "direct", or the literal meaning of the word. The connotative meaning of the word is implied and not directly stated; the connotative meaning is often associated with emotion and feeling about the typical context of the word.

Derivative of a Word

The derivative of a word is the final product after a word has undergone a change from its original form. For example, the word *fruit* refers to seed-containing products of a tree or plant that are often consumed by humans. If a prefix or suffix is added onto the root word *fruit*, the meaning of the word is changed. The suffix *-ful* added onto *fruit* to form the word *fruitful* would mean "full of fruit" or, more accurately, "abundant growth". Note that the meaning of the derivative, or final word form, changed from the meaning of the root word. If a word has been changed from its original form, it can have an entirely different meaning based on what prefixes or suffixes have been added onto the root word.

Using Specialized Reference Materials to Determine the Pronunciation of a Word

A print or digital dictionary can be used as a means to find the correct pronunciation of words. The dictionary will have a **phonetic** spelling that uses symbols to show how to correctly pronounce the words.

EXAMPLE

This chart shows three common symbols used in phonetic spellings of words along with a word the phoneme appears in

ʊ	ə	ŋ
good	teacher	sing

Use Context to Clarify Word Meaning

FINDING WORD MEANINGS

Readers of all levels will encounter words that they have either never seen or that they have seen before but still don't know what it means. The best way to define a word in **context** is to look for nearby words that can assist in learning the meaning of the word.

CONTEXT CLUES

Context clues are hints about the meaning of a word. They are the words or phrases in the sentence or sentences before and after a new or unfamiliar word. Context clues give the reader an idea about what a word means. A context clue may also contain words that help define the new word or an example of what the new word means. A context clue in the form of an example may contain the words including 'such as', a dash, or a colon before stated information.

Using context clues to figure out meaning can be helpful when learning a new set of vocabulary words or reading a difficult text. The dictionary definition of a word can always be looked up to double-check intended meaning.

Review Video: Reading Comprehension: Using Context Clues
Visit mometrix.com/academy and enter code: 613660

SYNONYMS AND ANTONYMS

When you understand how words relate to each other, you will discover more in a passage. This is explained by understanding **synonyms** (words that mean the same thing) and **antonyms** (words that mean the opposite of one another). As an example, *dry* and *arid* are synonyms, and *dry* and *wet* are antonyms.

RELATIONSHIPS BETWEEN WORDS

The relationships between words can often enlighten a reader as to their meaning. For instance, you may come across the word "colossal" and not understand what it means, but then you are told that it means the opposite of "little," giving you a good clue to its meaning. The same is true of synonyms. If someone said a synonym for "minuscule" is "tiny," you would understand the meaning of the word at once. Analogies can also be useful for understanding the meaning of words. If you are told that "foot" is to "toe" as "paw" is to "pad," then you get an idea of what a pad is from the analogy.

EXAMPLE 1

Determine the meaning of *cordial* in the following excerpt.

> The salesperson smiled when the couple came into the store. She told them to take their time in choosing a ring. She chatted with them about their future plans. She was the most *cordial* salesperson they had ever met.

The excerpt states that the salesperson smiled. It says that she told them to take their time and that she chatted with them. Obviously, the word *cordial* has a positive meaning based on these context clues. They seem to like the salesperson. She seems very pleasant. If you put the word "pleasant" in place of *cordial*, the sentences make sense. Through this process it is possible to use context clues to help the reader understand the meaning of an unknown word. The same process can be used to decipher the meanings of unknown expressions or sayings.

EXAMPLE 2

Read the sentence and explain the meaning of *sense of foreboding:*

> All day long Ron kept thinking about Sue. For some unknown reason he was worried about her. He had a strong *sense of foreboding* that something was about to go wrong in Sue's city. Then he heard about the earthquake there. Luckily Sue was not injured.

To figure out the meaning of the phrase *sense of foreboding*, the reader needs to look for context clues in just the same way the reader would do to figure out the meaning of a single word. The excerpt says that Ron was "worried" about Sue for "some unknown reason." It also says that he felt that "something was going to go wrong in Sue's city." Ron also heard about an earthquake taking place in Sue's city. A "sense of foreboding" must mean that Ron had an idea that something bad was going to happen. The context clues help the reader figure out the meaning of the phrase.

EXPERIENCE TO DETERMINE WORD MEANING

The more words a person is exposed to, the greater their vocabulary will become. By reading on a regular basis, a person can increase the number of ways they have seen a word in context. Based on experience, a person can recall how a word was used in the past and apply that knowledge to a new context.

For example, a person may have seen the word *gull* used to mean a bird that is found near the seashore. However, a *gull* can also be a person who is easily tricked. If the word is used in context in reference to a character, the reader can recognize that the character is being called a bird that is not seen as extremely intelligent. Using what the reader knows about a word can be useful when making comparisons or figuring out the meaning of a new use of a word, as in figurative language, idioms, analogies, and multiple-meaning words.

EXAMPLE 3

Using experience, determine the definition of the multiple-meaning word *basin* in the following sentence:

> The *basin* had filled with water over the summer months, so that the rocky bottom was no longer visible to the casual hiker.

A *basin* can be either a bowl filled with water or a depression in the earth. Looking at the context of the word in the sentence, the second definition is correct in this case. Knowing multiple definitions of a word can help when figuring out which definition applies in a sentence. If the definition of a word is not known, however, look at the context of the word. In the example, the reader knows that the *basin* had to be deep enough to fill with water. The reader also knows that the bottom of the *basin* had been filled with rock, and that the location is outdoors. Hikers are normally able to see the bottom of the *basin*, so it must be a large depression in the earth.

Substitution to Find Meaning

One way to find out if you have figured out the correct meaning of a new word is to substitute the meaning for the word. Using the example for *basin*, if the reader substituted in "depression in the earth," the sentence would read

> The "depression in the earth" had filled with water over the summer months, so that the rocky bottom was no longer visible to the casual hiker.

This is a way for the reader to confirm that they have used the context clues in the sentence correctly.

Words with Multiple Meanings

Some words are spelled exactly the same but have different meanings in different contexts. One needs to use the context of the situation to determine the correct meaning of the word in each case. Often, these words can be used as either a noun or a verb and their grammatical usage determines the meaning.

A **homonym** is defined as a word that has more than one meaning, but is spelled and pronounced the same for all of them.

For example, the word *degree* has at least three different meanings, depending on the situation in which the word is used: (a) a *degree* is the incremental measurement of temperature; (b) a *degree* is a title awarded upon graduation from college; and (c) *degree* can mean the extent or amount of something. Here are three different sentences, each using one of these meanings of the word *degree*:

1. You probably don't notice a difference when the temperature rises one *degree*.
2. The employer is only willing to hire someone with a *degree* in mathematics.
3. It was hard to tell the *degree* to which he really cared about the outcome.

Homophones are words that are pronounced the same, but may be spelled differently. An example of two homophones would be *heir* (someone due to inherit an estate) and *air* (the invisible substance people breathe).

Homographs are words that are spelled the same, but may be pronounced differently. An example of a homograph is the word *row*, which is pronounced one way when used to mean a horizontal grouping and is pronounced another way when used to mean an argument.

Using Roots to Determine Word Meaning

Affixes and Roots

A **root word** is a word that can be added onto. An **affix** is a prefix or suffix that is added onto a root word. Often, the affixes in the English language come from Latin or Greek origins. A **prefix** is added to the beginning of a root word and a **suffix** is added to the end of a root word.

For example, the word "inscription" is made up of three sections. The root *script* means "write" or "writing." There are two affixes in the word. The prefix *in-* can mean various things such as "not," but also "on." In this case it means "on." The suffix *-tion* means "action" or "process." So, put together, the word "inscription" means "the act of writing on." Studying roots and affixes is important because it allows you to decode words you might not otherwise understand with relative ease.

COMMON PREFIXES

Prefix	Meaning	Example
dis-	not	<u>dis</u>agree (not agree)
im-	not	<u>im</u>possibly (not possible)
in-	in, into, not	<u>in</u>justice (not just)
mis-	wrongly	<u>mis</u>spell (to spell wrongly)
non-	not	<u>non</u>paid (not paid)
pre-	before	<u>pre</u>view (to view before)
sub-	under	<u>sub</u>merge (to sink below the surface)
super-	over or greater than	<u>super</u>human (greater than a regular human
trans-	across, through, or change	<u>trans</u>late (to write or say in a different language)

COMMON SUFFIXES

Suffix	Meaning	Example
-able	can be done	like<u>able</u> (can be liked)
-er	a person connected with	teach<u>er</u> (a person connected with teaching)
-it/ity	state of	activ<u>ity</u> (state of being active)
-ful	full of	wonder<u>ful</u> (full of wonder)
-ive	cause to, tend to, or doing	creat<u>ive</u> (a person who tends to make new things or think of new ideas)
-ness	state of being	dark<u>ness</u> (being dark)
-ology	study of	bi<u>ology</u> (study of life)
-y	characterized by	cloud<u>y</u> (characterized by clouds)

LATIN ROOT WORDS

Latin Root	Meaning	Example
audi	hear	audible (able to be heard)
circ	round	circuit (a movement that starts and finishes at the same place)
dict	say	dictate (say or read aloud)
gen	to birth	generation (a group of people born and living at about the same time)
manu	hand	manicure (treatment of the hands, often involving painting the nails)
pac	peace	pacifist (a person who believes that war and violence cannot be justified)
vid / vis	to see	invisible (cannot be seen)

GREEK ROOT WORDS

Root	Meaning	Example
auto	self	automobile (a self-propelled vehicle)
geo	earth or ground	geography (study of the earth)
graph	writing	graphic (art, especially involving drawing or lettering)
meter	measure	thermometer (an instrument for measuring temperature)
photo	light	photon (a small particle of light)

EXAMPLE

Use knowledge of affixes to figure out the meaning of the word *mournful* in the following sentence:

> "Well, it being away in the night and stormy, and all so mysterious-like, I felt just the way any other boy would a felt when I see that wreck laying there so *mournful* and lonesome in the middle of the river." (From *The Adventures of Huckleberry Finn* by Mark Twain).

Mourn means to grieve for something, while *-ful* refers to being "full of". Putting the two components together, *mournful* means "full of grief or sadness". This definition makes sense in the context of the sentence. The "wreck" in the sentence is sad looking because it is in the river by itself.

When trying to determine the meaning of a word, always look for a root word and any prefixes or suffixes that have been added on to the root word. If a component of a word is not familiar, decipher what is clear about the word, then look at the word as used in context.

Main Idea and Supporting Details

Main Idea and Supporting Details

The main idea in a passage is usually located in the first paragraph or two of text. Having the main idea near the beginning of the passage allows the author to grab the reader's attention and let them know what the rest of the passage will discuss.

To find the main idea in a passage, there are questions the reader can ask while reading: What is this passage about? What does the author want the reader to know about the topic? The supporting details will provide evidence that the main idea is correct and are found in the body of a passage. The supporting details often provide examples of the main idea.

For example, a passage may contain the main idea: "Ellis Island was an entry-point to America for many immigrants during the Industrial Revolution." A supporting detail for the main idea may be "Immigrants were examined for contagious diseases at Ellis Island before being granted entry to America."

Review Video: Thesis Statements
Visit mometrix.com/academy and enter code: 691033

Example 1

Determine the main idea the following sentence tells the reader and indicate what details support the main idea:

> Her breath billowed out in clouds of white and disappeared into the quiet air.

The main idea is what the author wants the reader to understand about the text. Details help to explain or support that main idea. A main idea usually states the point of an entire essay, article, or book, but can be simply stated in one sentence. The main idea in the sentence above is that a girl is outside in the cold. Details to support this statement include the word 'her,' showing that the character is a girl, and 'clouds of white,' which indicate that the air is cold. In order to conclude that the girl is out in the cold, the reader needs to understand that breath can be seen when the air is cold.

Supporting Details

Provide evidence and backing for the main point. All texts contain details, but they are only classified as supporting details when they serve to reinforce some larger point. Supporting details are most commonly found in informative and persuasive texts. In some cases, they will be clearly indicated with words like **for example** or **for instance**, or they will begin with words like **first**, **second**, and **last**. However, these special words are not a requirement. As a reader, it is important to consider whether the author's supporting details really back up his or her main point. Supporting details can be factual and correct but still not relevant to the author's point. Sometimes, supporting details can seem important but they might not support the main idea in the story well because they are based on opinion that cannot be proven.

Example 2

Decide whether the following sentence is the main point or a supporting point of a text, and state where the information would be placed in an outline:

> One type of horseback riding, bareback horseback riding, involves sitting on a moving horse without a saddle and grasping the horse's mane.

This sentence is a supporting point, with the main point of the entire text likely about horseback riding in general. As a supporting point, this sentence would go further down in an outline, next to any numeral after numeral I. This sentence can be followed by additional sub-points that further explain the concept of bareback horseback riding. When a supporting point is used to clarify a main point or topic, the supporting point helps to break the topic down into smaller pieces.

Opposite Point of View

After identifying the main idea, readers can increase their understanding of the text if they think about what the opposite point of view would be.

Read the following topic sentence. Describe what the opposite point of view would include:

> The new bike path at the public park provides families in the community with a safe opportunity to get some fresh air on the weekends.

This topic sentence could be taken in several different directions. The main focus of the sentence is that the bike path is safe and allows for families to get out and enjoy some fresh air on the weekends. The opposite point of view may state that the new bike path is unsafe and the air is polluted. An example of a topic sentence with the opposite point of view may state: The new bike path at Primer School is unsafe for families in the community to travel on the weekends and goes through a polluted area.

When looking for the main point in a sentence, look for keywords that define the sentence. In the sentence about the bike path, we know that the path is new, seems safe, and has fresh air. By changing around these keywords, the entire meaning of the sentence can be shifted.

Central Argument

A central argument is the main point of a book or essay. It is the author's opinion and is usually the reason they are writing the book or essay. It can be structured in several different ways including argument by cause and effect, argument by analogy, and argument by authority. When an author uses argument by cause and effect, they are trying to convince the reader that a certain cause will produce a specific effect. An argument by analogy uses perceived similarities as a basis in order to argue for some further similarity that has not yet been observed. Finally, an argument by authority is being used when an author argues for something on the basis of someone's authority. This can be a positive thing when the referenced person's authority involves having a great deal of knowledge on the subject, but would be considered a logical fallacy if the person's authority is unrelated to the subject of the argument.

Themes

THEME

The **theme** of a story is a unifying idea that is used throughout the text; it can take the form of a common setting, idea, symbol, design, or recurring event. The theme of a story may vary according to place, time, and characters, but theme is often based on common human experience. A plot line is built around the theme of a story. Most themes are about life, society, or human nature. The theme is often why a passage is written. It helps give a passage unity. The theme is created through the development of the story. The events of a story help shape the kind of theme the passage. A theme is not usually stated explicitly. The reader **infers** the theme from the topic, information, or plot of a passage.

For example, a series of events in a story may be based upon people being willing to trust the actions of others. The story may be centered on why people need to trust others in order to carry out important actions. For example, a character may trust that a bus driver will stay on the road while the bus driver, in turn, trusts that the passengers stay in their seats so that they do not distract him.

The theme of a story is not the same as the topic of a story. The topic is what the story is about, but the theme is what a reader is meant to learn. When readers are discussing theme, they can determine both theme topics as well as theme statements.

Theme topics are broad ideas that apply to the text. Examples include:

- Love changes people
- Man versus man
- Man versus nature
- Man versus himself
- Fate versus free will
- Triumph over adversity
- Coming of age
- The importance of friendship
- Good vs. evil
- The circle of life

Theme statements are specific ideas that must be written in sentence form, and usually contain the name of the work and the author. Examples include:

- In *The City of Ember* by Jeanne DuPrau, the author shows how acts of courage can bring positive changes to the world.
- The author of *Uglies*, Scott Westerfeld, introduces readers to a futuristic world where the idea of what makes a person beautiful is explored.

EXAMPLE 1

Tell why the theme of the following excerpt should be "Overconfidence can lead to a fall."

> Bella was happy. She auditioned for the starring role in the school play and she felt sure she'd got the part. Afterwards, she told her friends she would be starring in the play. But on Tuesday when the director said they had offered the part to Sara Goodwin, she started crying.

The excerpt tells the story of a girl who has an audition and thinks she got the starring role. She is so confident that she even tells her friends that she has the part. But then she learns that the role was offered to someone else and she starts to cry. She was overly confident about her success and was subsequently devastated when she learned of her failure, and that is the lesson of the story. If you are overly confident you may have a fall. That is the theme of the story. A theme is the lesson that a story teaches. This particular theme is found often in literature. A theme is not stated in a passage: the reader must deduce it from the plot of the story.

EXAMPLE 2

Determine the theme of the following short paragraph:

> Matt had spent a lot of time preparing for his first babysitting experience. Matt stayed fully attentive to his young cousin, Toby, while he played outside. When his aunt returned, Matt was proud to report that all had gone well. He had acted in the adult role.

The short paragraph shown here is a coming of age story. This means that the protagonist goes through some kind of experience that changes him or her from a child into an adult. By preparing to care for his cousin Toby and keeping him safe while his aunt was away, Matt became more of an adult and less of a child. Taking care of someone else is an adult thing to do and Matt was successful. This was a defining moment in his life.

CHARACTERS AND THEME

What a character says either to another character or about a situation may help the reader determine the theme of the text by revealing what a character is thinking or what he may do. Dialogue in the text can also help the reader determine the theme of the story by showing what the character intends to do in the future. For instance, as you read, ask yourself if a character is doing something wrong and, if so, ask yourself if the character is punished at the end of a story.

UNIVERSAL THEMES

Some themes are fairly common. These themes are called **universal themes** and they suggest things about life, society, and human nature. If a reader is trying to decide whether a theme is universal or not, they must consider whether the theme they have identified can be applied to other works as well. Some examples of universal theme topics are:

GOOD VERSUS EVIL

- The universal theme of a small number of people invested in doing good works becoming a powerful force against those doing evil works can be seen in multiple texts, including the *Harry Potter* series by J.K. Rowling, *The Hunger Games* by Suzanne Collins, and *Cinder* by Marissa Meyer.

CHANGE VERSUS TRADITION

- *The Giver* by Lois Lowry, the *Divergent* series by Veronica Roth, and *Children of Eden* by Joey Graceffa all reveal the universal theme of the ongoing struggle for societies to welcome change rather than being stuck in tradition.

MAN VERSUS MAN

- Learning that people are capable of committing horrifying acts against other people is a universal theme evident in *The Boy in the Striped Pajamas* by John Boyne, *A Long Walk to Water* by Linda Sue Park, and *All the Light We Cannot See* by Anthony Doerr.

Paraphrasing and Summarizing

Paraphrasing and Summarizing

Paraphrasing and summarizing are two ways readers can work to understand what they read. Both involve reading a text and recalling the main points in an accurate way, but they differ in several ways.

How to Paraphrase	How to Summarize
State the message in the text in the reader's own words, while keeping the original meaning of the text Take all of the original ideas and word them in a way that the reader can better understand Put what the reader has read into their own words, rephrasing what the author has written	State main points of the text clearly and to-the-point. Take information and state it simply, in a much shorter form. Put information in a short form that keeps the main points of the whole text. Do not include many details, just the main idea of the text

Paraphrasing is often done for individual ideas, while summarizing is done for an entire block of text or ideas. Often times, a summary can be done in just one sentence, boiling down the author's words into just main idea.

Review Video: Summarizing Text
Visit mometrix.com/academy and enter code: 172903

Summarizing Literature to Support Comprehension

When reading literature, especially demanding works, summarizing helps readers identify important information and organize it in their minds. They can also identify themes, problems, and solutions, and can sequence the story. Readers can summarize before, during, and after they read. They should use their own words, as they do when describing a personal event or giving directions. Previewing a text's organization before reading by examining the book cover, table of contents, and illustrations also aids summarizing. So does making notes of key words and ideas in a graphic organizer while reading. Graphic organizers are another useful method; readers skim the text to determine main ideas and then narrow the list with the aid of the organizer. Unimportant details should be omitted in summaries. Summaries can include description, problem-solution, comparison-contrast, sequence, main ideas, and cause-and-effect.

Evaluation of Summaries

A summary of a literary passage is a condensation in the reader's own words of the passage's main points. Several guidelines can be used in evaluating a summary. The summary should be complete yet concise. It should be accurate, balanced, fair, neutral, and objective, excluding the reader's own opinions or reactions. It should reflect in similar proportion how much each point summarized was covered in the original passage. Summary writers should include tags of attribution, like "Macaulay argues that" to reference the original author whose ideas are represented in the summary. Summary writers should not overuse quotations: they should only quote central concepts or phrases they cannot precisely convey in words other than those of the original author. Another aspect in evaluating a summary is whether it can stand alone as a coherent, unified composition. In addition, evaluation of a summary should include whether its writer has cited the original source of the passage so that readers can find it.

Example Summary

Read the following paragraph and then give a one sentence summary statement:

> When choosing a pet, people need to think about what type of home they can offer the animal. For example, a small apartment might not be a good fit for a large dog, but could be a comfortable home for a kitten. A house that has a big yard would be great for a puppy, but a rabbit does not need a large yard.

In order to summarize, one has to identify the main idea and any supporting ideas in the author's work. The summary is an overview of the author's paragraph and will tell what it is about without getting into any of the details. The summary needs to be broad enough to cover all of the information in the author's paragraph. Here is a possible summary statement for the above paragraph:

> People need to consider a number of factors, particularly the available space they have, when choosing a pet.

Example Paraphrasing

Read the following sentences and then paraphrase the material:

> The government is debating a new health care system for our country. The Senate and the House of Representatives have both passed bills; now they need to resolve these two bills into one bill that a majority can agree on.

When paraphrasing information, one needs to read carefully and pay attention to details, then put the material away and write or tell it in their own words. One does not want to look at the material while paraphrasing to avoid plagiarizing by accident. Here is one example of a way to paraphrase the sentences:

> Our government is trying to adopt a new health care system. The Senate has passed a bill and so has the House of Representatives. Their bills are different so now they have to compromise on one bill that can be passed.

Objective Summary

An objective summary of an informational text tells what the main idea of the text is and includes the important details. It tells what the text is mostly about and includes the most important supporting details. A summary should not include too much information; it is not a paraphrase of the information. It is important to select only the most important details to include. A summary should also be objective. This is achieved by focusing on the main idea rather than any opinions that might be in the text but that are not related to the main idea. It would also not include any personal opinions on the subject.

Example 1

Read the summary and explain how to improve it.

> Edgar Degas was a great artist who broke with tradition and became an Impressionist. His paintings and sculptures are included in the collections of major museums everywhere. In his forties, his vision became poor and he worked more on sculptures because he could feel them. He died in 1917 at the age of 83. His father was a banker.

This summary is quite good. It has a main idea and includes some of the important details. The main idea is that Degas was a great artist. Supporting details include that his paintings and sculpture are included in collections of major museums as well as the fact that he had poor vision and turned to sculpting because he could feel the sculptures. While the information about his death is not perhaps the most important, it is of interest that he lived to the age of 83. The one glaring error with the summary is that it mentions the fact that his father was a banker. This does not directly relate to the main idea. It is not a supporting detail and is unimportant to the central thesis of the passage. It should be deleted.

Example 2

Read the summary and discuss how it could be improved.

> This story is about a man and a woman who moved to the West many years ago. There was a lot of information about covered wagons or "prairie schooners," as they called them. I liked the story because of that.

The summary tells the main idea of the story, but it doesn't include the details of what happens in the story. It does not include the main characters and what they did or what challenges they faced. It does not summarize the plot. Another problem with the summary is that it is not objective; it is subjective. The writer describes what he thinks about the story. But personal opinions have no place in an objective summary of a story. To improve it, the writer should remove his personal opinion and add descriptions of who was in the story, what important things happened to them, and how the story ended.

Plot Elements

Linear Plot Development

The storyline of any text is also called a **plot**. The characters and events in the story determine what the plot will be. When events occur in a **linear** way, the story is generally told in chronological order and the order of events make sense. In texts with linear plots, readers may find a **plot line** useful as they try to put the events in the text in order and determine the relationships between events.

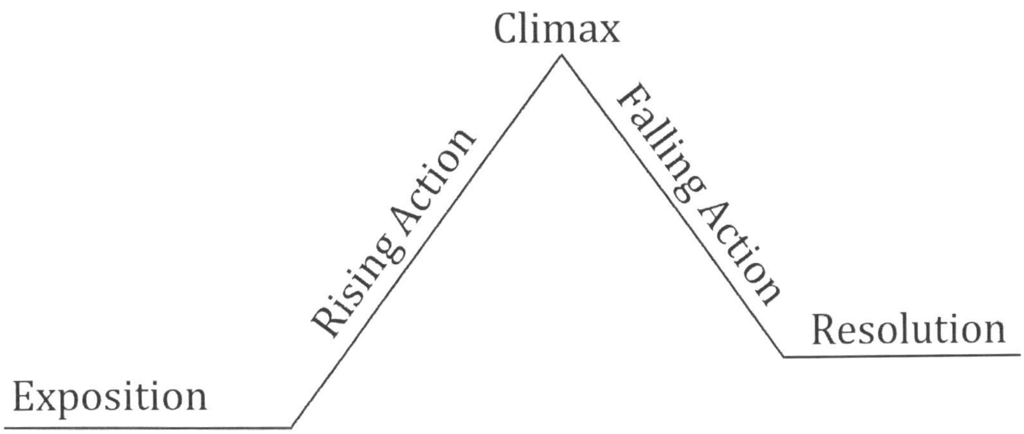

Linear plots will begin with **exposition**, which introduces the characters and the setting of the story. The plot will continue to develop as new ideas and events centered on the main conflict in the story are revealed, which is called the **rising action**. The action in the story will rise until a **climax** is reached within the conflict. The climax can also be referred to as the turning point in the story, since the climax is where each character makes an important decision. After the climax, the action starts to wind down during the **falling action**. At this point, the characters begin to follow the paths they chose in during climax. The events of the story reach **resolution** in some way by the end of the story. Some conflicts are left open-ended, so that the reader is left to decide what really happened at the end of the story. Keep in mind that not all resolutions are happy or peaceful.

Identifying the Main Conflict

An important part of analyzing the plot of a passage is identifying the **main conflict**. There will likely be many smaller conflicts in the story, but there will be one main problem that influences the characters and events. To identify the main conflict, first look at who the main character is. Now ask yourself what they want. They may want to something to happen or not happen, another character to do or not do something, or to confront or avoid a problem, among other things. Once you know what they want, now ask yourself what is standing in the character's way. It may be a person, an event, or something less tangible like the passing of time. Combining what the main character wants and why they do not currently have leaves the reader with a summary of the main conflict.

Example 1

Read the following sentence from *The Call of the Wild* by Jack London and describe the main conflict in the sentence. Explain how the conflict may be resolved.

> The breaking down of discipline likewise affected the dogs in their relations with one another.

Based on the information in the sentence, an event has caused the dogs, the characters in the story, to not follow their regular routine. The sentence indicates that there has been a breaking down of discipline which is affecting how the dogs relate to each other. In order to solve this conflict, discipline needs to be restored. However, in order to return to previous relations between the dogs, any problems that are in the way of conflict resolution need to be taken care of. The word *likewise* means *also*, which tells the reader that other parts of the story are being affected besides the relations between the dogs.

Non-Linear Plot Development

Some texts contain a **non-linear plot**, which means the plot is not told in chronological order, or is not told from "beginning to end" in one straight line. There are several devices that authors can use to make their plot non-linear, some of which are

- **Foreshadowing** -the author gives the reader hints early on in a work about something that will become clearer (or more important) later on.
- **Flashback** -the author shows the reader an event that happened in the past to explain something about the present.
- **Subplot** -a side story, usually about a supporting character, is told along with the main story. Sometimes subplots occur within flashbacks.
- **Parallel plot** -two stories are told alongside each other, often narrated by two different characters in alternating chapters. The events in the stories usually end up overlapping or coming together at some point, most often the climax of the text.

Setting in Story

Setting

The setting is where a story takes place. The setting of a story may stay the same for the entire story, or change as events in the story unfold. For example, an entire story may take place in one room or cross continents as the reader follows the characters along on a trail of events.

The setting of a story is described by the author in terms of what it looks like, how the character feels, and anything else that is happening at that location at the time. For example, a character may be caught on a doorstep on a cold, rainy day. The character may feel frustrated as they shiver in the doorway, waiting for the heavy rain to let up a bit.

Shaping a Character with Setting or Plot

The setting of a story shapes character because it helps to define the situation that a character finds herself in. A character is limited to the setting of a story. For example, if a story takes place in a cold environment filled with snow and ice, this is certain to impact what actions a character can and will take. Frequently, the setting changes the way characters behave based on time. For example, the character of a woman who is a single mother in 1920 would be seen and behave very differently than a single mother in 2020.

Example

Read the excerpt and determine how the setting influences the character in this excerpt.

> She had swum too far out. The waves were higher than she thought. She was struggling hard to get to shore. She wondered if she would make it. She thought of her childhood. Had she been right to run away from home, she wondered? Just then, a lifeguard grabbed her and helped her to shore.

The setting of the ocean and the high waves creates a conflict in the character. She is worried. She thinks about her childhood and her parents. She doesn't know if she will make it to shore. This is how the setting affects the character in this excerpt. Without the high waves and the struggle, she would not become so worried and start to think about her past. She probably would not have questioned herself. This is an example of how a setting influences a character. If the waves had not been high, there probably would not have been a struggle or any self-searching of the swimmer's past.

PERCEPTION OF A STORY BASED ON SETTING

The setting of a story can allow the reader to draw on personal experience about where the story takes place. If a story takes place on a farm, the reader will likely picture a rural, peaceful setting, which may go along with (or be in contrast to) the actual plot of the story. For example, a reader would not expect a scary story to occur on a farm on a sunny day. Conversely, a reader may view a dark subway as a dangerous place, while the plot of a story set there may be based on a very calm series of events. When an author is crafting a story, they need to consider what the audience may already think about a particular setting in order to properly present the events of a story for greatest impact.

HISTORICAL AND CULTURAL SETTING

Historical context influences literature in a number of ways. The style of the author's writing can be impacted by the historical period during which it was written (e.g., Dickens wrote at a time when authors were paid by the word; this is why his novels are so long). Obviously, the setting of the book includes its historical context. In addition, dialect may be a function of the historical period of the book. When a reader understands the historical context of a particular book, he or she can have a deeper understanding of the novel. Knowing about the time period during which the author wrote, as well as the time period discussed in the novel, helps the reader understand some of the author's choices, including character motivations.

EXAMPLE

Slavery used to be the norm in Southern states. One of the major ways in which the historical context of slavery impacted literature coming out of the South was the birth of the slave narrative. Slaves wanted to have their experiences documented. After the Civil War, former slaves wrote their stories. These slave narratives have given historians valuable firsthand accounts of life in the South. From a literary perspective, slave narratives are one of the most important genres of African-American writing. Slavery influenced literature by delving into themes of power, racial injustice, and equality. Literature from this time period can help the reader better understand the perspectives and experiences of the slaves themselves, as well as the slave holders.

Characters and their Roles in Story

CONFLICT

The conflict in a text occurs when something goes wrong. The are many different kinds of conflicts, but they often occur either because of **external** forces that characters can't control (like catching a cold) or because of **interactions** between characters (like arguing over who to invite). Usually, the conflict is solved by the end of the story.

Review Video: Conflict
Visit mometrix.com/academy and enter code: 559550

EXAMPLE 1

Read the following sentence and explain the main conflict between the two characters:

> Joe stared angrily at Jamie's retreating back as Jamie raced away down the field with Joe's soccer ball.

The main conflict in the sentence is that Jamie has Joe's soccer ball. There may be additional conflicts between the two characters, but from the evidence shown in the sentence, Joe seems to be angry that Jamie has his soccer ball.

In any story, a conflict may be minor and only affect part of the story, or be the main focus of the story. An entire story may entail solving a conflict between characters. In the context of the sentence, it is not clear whether or not the entire story will revolve around Jamie taking Joe's soccer ball. However, the current conflict is based upon that information in the sentence.

EXAMPLE 2

Read the following sentence and analyze how the problem can be resolved:

> Jason had homework in five subjects over the weekend, but he also had a basketball game to attend on Saturday evening.

The main problem, or conflict in the story, is that Jason has multiple obligations. He needs to complete work for school over the weekend, but he also has to, or wants to, attend a basketball game. In order to solve the problem, Jason needs to figure out how long each obligation will take. He also needs to take into account that time will be spent on daily activities, such as eating and sleeping. Once Jason figures out how much time it will take to complete homework for each subject and how much time the basketball game will take (including preparation time), he can figure out how to divide up his weekend hours. For example, Jason may say that the homework for one subject will take an hour to complete, while the homework for the other four subjects will take half an hour each. That means that Jason will need to set aside at least three hours of time to complete homework over the weekend.

EXAMPLE 3

Read the following sentence from *The Call of the Wild* by Jack London and describe the main conflict in the sentence and how the conflict may be resolved:

> The breaking down of discipline likewise affected the dogs in their relations with one another.

Based on the information in the sentence, an event has caused the dogs, the characters in the story, to not follow their regular routine. The sentence indicates that there has been a breaking down of discipline which is affecting how the dogs relate to each other. In order to solve this conflict, discipline needs to be restored in the story. There may be another conflict that needs to be resolved in order to re-establish discipline. However, in order to return to previous relations between the dogs, any problems that are in the way of conflict resolution need to be taken care of. The word "likewise" means also, which tells the reader that other avenues are being affected in the story besides the relations between the dogs.

CHARACTER RELATIONSHIPS AND CHANGES

Characters can change in a multitude of ways throughout a story; however, there are main aspects of a character that change. A character's identifying characteristics, such as personality or behavior traits, may change as the result of a prominent event in the story, current motivations, and conflicts. As conflicts change or are resolved, a character may no longer be motivated by striving toward a goal that was previously important to them. As the plot of a story moves along, characters can constantly change in relation to events that occur. Relationships between characters and the points of view of characters may change throughout a story as well.

Each story will have many different types of characters and each of these characters will have a different relationship with other characters. Stories usually have a protagonist, antagonist, and a variety of other characters including round, flat, and stock characters.

Protagonist

The main character in a drama, movie, novel, or other fictional text. The author portrays the protagonist in a way that the audience is most like to identify with themselves. The protagonist is generally undertaking some type of personal challenge throughout the story. The author writes the story so that the reader becomes aware of the protagonist's emotions and is generally able to empathize with the personal challenge.

Antagonist

The character that actively opposes the protagonist by trying to prevent them from succeeding. The antagonist is usually presented in such a way as to make the audience dislike them, and want them to fail at stopping the protagonist. The protagonist and antagonist oppose each other, so their relationship is almost always one of dislike.

Flat Character

Does not have any substantial changes throughout the story. They stay the same despite the conflict, and do not learn any lessons. They are usually minor characters that might interact with the main character in some way.

Round Character

Major characters in the story that will be more fully developed than other minor characters. They will usually encounter some type of conflict that they must overcome, and usually learn a lesson about life or themselves along the way.

Stock Characters

Often get their characteristics and mannerisms from stereotypes of people that are widely recognized. These types of characters are often repeated and well-known. Readers should be aware that stereotypes are rarely accurate in reality, and are generally intended to be humorous or dramatic. Some examples are evil stepmothers, unintelligent blondes, rude athletes, and loyal servants.

Driving the Action

There are many ways in which the action of a story may be driven. Dialogue is one of them. What a character says either to another character or about a situation may propel the action by revealing what a character is thinking or what he may do. Similarly, what a character says will tell the audience what he is like. His manner of speaking, what he says, and how he says it are all clues to his personality. Dialogue can also provoke a decision by showing what the character intends to do in the future. Incidents in a story also propel the action because the plot is made up of events that build on events. Incidents such as a confrontation could reveal aspects of a character or provoke a decision.

Example 4

Read the excerpt and tell how this incident propels the action of the story and provokes a decision.

> It was a perfect day it seemed, until Sam saw the thunderheads roll in. He knew that it would be dangerous to be in a rowboat in the middle of the lake during a thunder and lightning storm. Suddenly the sky became darker and he heard a clap of thunder.

This incident certainly propels the action of the story. It would appear that Sam is in a rowboat in the middle of the lake having a lovely time when he hears a clap of thunder. He realizes that a lake is a dangerous place to be so this event means that Sam must take action. What that action is would be of interest to the reader because it will help form the plot of the story. The incident also forces Sam to make a decision about what he should do. This will help the reader better understand Sam as a character.

Character Trait

The traits of a character may include how they act and physical characteristics; a character trait is a behavior or physical characteristic that is unique to a specific character. For example, a character may be outgoing, which means he or she likes to talk a lot, or they may have bright red hair. These are both character traits.

An author uses character traits to describe a character in a story and help the reader to learn more about how the character acts and what they look like. By comparing the character traits in a story, the reader can see similarities and differences between characters. The author includes character traits to help the reader understand why a character may act a certain way in the story. For example, a character who is shy may not want to talk with a lot of people in a new classroom, but a character who is outgoing may want to talk with many people.

An author typically provides many details about a character so that the reader can learn more about the character's traits, motivations, relationships, and any conflicts they may have in the story. The traits of a character may include how they act and how they look. Characters are often motivated by things that have already happened in their life or how they feel about a topic. The author will often give the reader enough information about the character so that the reader can figure out why the character responds to a situation in a certain way. The author will also often give details about the relationships between characters and points they may conflict on. For example, a character may be good friends with another character; however, the two characters may disagree on where to play outside if one character likes being near the water and the other character does not.

Example 5

Read the following description of a character and decide, logically, whether the character is likely to go hiking outdoors:

> Jeremy lived in a high-rise in Chicago. He was studious, and not very athletic. Jeremy preferred to stay indoors and read a book, rather than enjoy outdoor weather.

Based on the description of the character's traits, preferences, and personality, he is not likely to go hiking outdoors. The description indicates that the character prefers reading, rather than enjoying outdoor weather. In addition, the character lives in a tall building in the middle of a large city, in order for him to enjoy the outdoors, he would have to travel away from where he lives. The character is not likely to change his preferences. A situation may lead the character to go hiking, but he is not likely to initiate the action on his own. A description of a character that is likely to go hiking outdoors may include a preference for outdoor activity and living near trails.

Literary Devices

Point of View

An author may use first, second, or third person point of view in a text.

- First person point of view is written from the perspective of one character. Use of the pronouns 'I', 'me', 'we', and 'my' indicate that the author is using first person point of view.
- Second person point of view uses the pronoun 'you' when telling the story to another person. Second person point of view is the least commonly used point of view.
- Third person point of view tells a story from an all-knowing, or omniscient, perspective. The reader can get into the thoughts and points of view of multiple characters in a story when third person point of view is used.

Subjective and Objective Point of View

The point of view of a character or narrator can either be **subjective** or **objective**. When a character or narrator is describing a person, object, or idea using phrases that are based on opinions or motivated by feelings, their point of view is subjective. When they use phrases based on facts or something that can be proven, their point of view is objective. For example, if a character describes a person walking toward them and they say "Her shirt was a beautiful shade of yellow, which made her blonde hair shine even brighter" they are speaking in subjective point of view. The yellow color they think is beautiful could be someone else's least favorite color. If the same character described the situation objectively, they might say "As she walked by, I noticed her shirt was yellow and her hair was blonde." The narrator doesn't comment on his opinion of the color, just that it is factually yellow.

Example 1

Determine whether the following excerpt from Jordan Sonnenblick's novel *Drums, Girls & Dangerous Pie* is written using subjective or objective point of view

> 'Did you really JUST fall, Jeffrey?'
> Why does everybody in my family talk in these dramatic CAPITAL LETTERS all the time?
> Why am I the only calm one?

In this excerpt, the narrator's point of view is subjective. Steven describes himself as the "only calm one" in his family, and while he may honestly feel this way, it is a statement based on feelings, not on facts. Steven cannot prove that he is the only calm one, and a different member of the family would likely view the situation differently, which makes his point of view subjective.

Dramatic Irony

Dramatic irony refers to a situation when a character makes a remark about doing something that seems harmless in its context, but that the audience has more information about and realizes it could result in something unpleasant. This difference in knowledge can create suspense or humor depending on the circumstances. For instance, if a character says, "I will have a cup of tea now," and the audience knows that there is poison in the tea, it creates a situation that is suspenseful. That is an example of dramatic irony. The word "irony" comes from the Greek word for "dissembling" and it was used to describe what the Greeks thought was the gap between appearance and reality.

Verbal Irony and Puns

Verbal irony is a figure of speech which occurs when the intended meaning of a statement is different than, and usually the opposite of, what is said. It is often sarcastic in nature, as in the retort of the mother whose child is playing with her food and says, "Do I have to eat this food?" The mother simply says, "No, of course you don't have to eat it. Just eat it tomorrow when you are really hungry." The mother does not mean what she is actually saying, and is instead trying to make the point that if the child doesn't eat now, they will be extremely hungry later. A **pun** is a play on words, as seen in this example from Lewis Carroll's *Alice's Adventures in Wonderland*

> 'Mine is a long and a sad tale!' said the Mouse, turning to Alice, and sighing. 'It is a long tail, certainly,' said Alice, looking down with wonder at the Mouse's tail; 'but why do you call it sad?' And she kept on puzzling about it while the Mouse was speaking.

The author creates a pun using the words "tail" and "tale" to confuse Alice, and to entertain the reader.

Connecting to a Text

Making Connections to Enhance Comprehension

Reading involves thinking. For good comprehension, readers make text-to-self, text-to-text, and text-to-world connections. Making connections helps readers understand text better and predict what might occur next based on what they already know, such as how characters in the story feel or what happened in another text. Readers can make connections before, during, and after reading. Venn diagrams and other graphic organizers can help readers visualize connections.

Text-to-Self

Reading while looking for connections with the reader's life and experiences makes literature more personally relevant and meaningful to readers. Sentences showing text-to-self connections may begin with these examples

- This is similar to a time when...
- I empathize with this character because...
- The setting makes me think of...
- I experienced this same thing when...

Text-to-Text

Reading while looking for connections to other texts helps the reader learn to identify the way authors use genre, setting, characters, plot elements, literary structure and devices, and themes to create meaning. Authors can also **allude** to other works by quoting or referencing events from a well-known source. Sentences showing text-to-text connections may begin with these examples

- The character shares the same flaw as the character in...
- This is an allusion to the events in...
- The conflict in this story is similar to the conflict in...
- The relationship between the protagonist and antagonist is different than the one in...

Text-to-World

Reading while looking for connections to the world helps the reader begin to see literature as a reflection of real life and notice patterns in history and current events. Sentences showing text-to-world connections may begin with these examples

- The event in this story sounds like the event in history when…
- The actions of this character sound like the historical tale of…
- This is like what happened in real life when…
- I heard about this on the news when…

Making Inferences

Inference

An **inference** is a **conclusion** or generalization that the reader makes based on the information provided within a text. Certain facts are included to help a reader come to a specific conclusion. It is what the story may hint about, and what a reader can conclude as a result of what the author says in the passage. It is also the best guess that a reader can make based on what happened or was said or in a story. A good inference is based on or supported by details in the passage.

Readers may come to their own conclusion about a topic, or the author may state a conclusion at the end of a story. When readers are in the middle of a story, they can predict what will happen at the end of it based on the events that have occurred so far and the typical characteristics that have been presented by the author up to that point. A reader needs to consider all of the information that an author has presented, including the main point and supporting points, to make logical conclusions and inferences about the story.

For instance, if a passage says that Joan is holding her mouth and moaning, you might conclude, or **infer,** that she has a sore mouth or a toothache. You cannot be sure of this, but it is the best conclusion that you can reach using the information at hand. Inferences are considered **implicit information**. They are not found directly in a passage.

Review Video: Inference
Visit mometrix.com/academy and enter code: 379203

Example 1

An inference can be made about the character of the narrator based on the following excerpt from David Copperfield by Charles Dickens:

> My father's eyes had closed upon the light of this world six months, when mine opened on it. There is something strange to me…in the shadowy remembrance that I have of my first childish associations with his white grave-stone in the churchyard, and of the indefinable compassion I used to feel for it lying out alone there in the dark night, when our little parlour was warm and bright with fire and candle, and the doors of our house were - almost cruelly, it seemed to me sometimes - bolted and locked against it.

In order to make an inference, the reader must use clues from the passage to come to a conclusion. It is explicitly stated in the passage that David's father died before he was born. Based on the excerpt, the reader can infer that David Copperfield feels sadness over the loss of his father, even though he never knew him. This inference about David's character can be made using context clues from the passage: David feels "indefinable compassion" for his father's gravestone. The phrase "almost cruelly" indicates that David feels that his family is perhaps too harsh in their treatment of his father. He feels a connection to his father's gravestone and feels bad that the stone is left out in the cold when his house is warm.

EXAMPLE 2

An inference can be made about the character Pip based on the following excerpt from Great Expectations by Charles Dickens:

> I never had one hour's happiness in her society, and yet my mind all round the four-and-twenty hours was harping on the happiness of having her with me unto death.

In order to make an inference, the reader must use clues from the passage to come to a conclusion. This excerpt shows the reader Pip, who is thinking about a romantic relationship with a woman. The words "yet my mind all round the four and twenty hours" and "harping" lead the reader to infer that he has a crush on this woman and cannot get her out of his thoughts. Pip has never enjoyed her company, yet he dreams of their happiness together. From this, the reader can infer that Pip is unrealistic about romantic relationships.

EXAMPLE 3

Draw a conclusion based on the following sentence.

> New Orleans then was a mere huddle of buildings around Jackson Square; but with the purchase of the Louisiana territory from France, and the great influx of American enterprise that characterized the first quarter of the last century, development was working like yeast...

The reader needs to use prior experience and background information to draw an accurate conclusion about the sentence. The sentence describes how New Orleans grew after the "purchase of the Louisiana territory" and how "development was working like yeast". Yeast multiplies rapidly, so the reader can conclude that New Orleans was growing rapidly.

Using Evidence to Support a Response

TEXT EVIDENCE

The term **text evidence** refers to information included in a text that supports the main point of the paper. A reader can draw conclusions or generalizations based upon information found in a text, in which the author will deliberately include key points that serve as supporting details for the main point. For example, the main point of a paper may state: The average yearly rainfall in the city has risen by 2 inches per year in the past five years. The paper would go on to include the amount of rainfall for each month or season and any contributing factors that may be causing an increase in yearly rainfall. Additional facts, or text evidence to support the point that yearly rainfall is rising in the city would help to prove that the author's main point is correct. In fiction, details about characters, events, and setting can be both explicit and implicit.

Review Video: Textual Evidence
Visit mometrix.com/academy and enter code: 486236

EXPLICIT INFORMATION

Explicit information includes facts and statements that are found directly in a passage or a story. It is not information that is hinted at or information you need to make a conclusion about. Explicit information may be found in many forms; it can be contained in a quote as well as in a description. It can be found in dialogue and in actions. This information can sometimes be used to support an inference. The answers to questions about explicit information are found through careful reading of the text. Attention is given to important facts or other information.

EXAMPLE 1

Read the following excerpt and identify which information is explicit.

> In ancient times the value of an ox was the basis for the monetary systems of the Greeks, Assyrians, Mesopotamians, and the Egyptians. Each of these territories had their own currency. For instance, Egypt traded in gold and Greece in silver or copper.

All of the information in the excerpt is explicit. Nothing is hinted at. It says that the value of an ox was the basis for the monetary system for ancient Greeks, Assyrians, Mesopotamians, and the Egyptians. It adds that each of these territories had their own currency. It further informs that Egypt traded in gold and Greece in silver or copper. All of this information is factual. There are no opinions in the excerpt. There is nothing with which to make an inference.

IMPLICIT INFORMATION

Implicit information is information that is not directly stated in a text, but can be inferred from something that the author explicitly states. For instance, the author may say "Seth buys a new TV, laptop, and home theater system every year." From this the reader could infer several things. For instance, Seth probably likes electronics and has a lot of spending money.

EXAMPLE

Draw a conclusion based on the implicit information in the following sentence from *The Adventures of Tom Sawyer* by Mark Twain:

> He had discovered a great law of human action, without knowing it—namely, that in order to make a man or a boy covet a thing, it is only necessary to make the thing difficult to attain.

The reader can clearly see from the sentence that the character did not set out to learn something, but through an action, the character learned that people will want what is hard to attain. Although it's not explicitly stated, the reader can draw the conclusion that the character gained the experience of coveting (or desiring) something that was hard to get.

DRAWING CONCLUSIONS BASED ON TEXT EVIDENCE

Readers often need to use prior experience and background information to draw an accurate conclusion about the passage they are reading. Sometimes interpreting the information in a sentence can be difficult, especially if the reader is unfamiliar with some of the words used in a sentence. Looking at the words that the reader does understand in the sentence can help. By taking a pen or pencil and underlining important information in a sentence, the reader can better understand what the author is trying to say and draw a clearer conclusion from that.

EXAMPLE 1

Draw a conclusion based on the following sentence.

New Orleans then was a mere huddle of buildings around Jackson Square; but with the purchase of the Louisiana territory from France, and the great influx of American enterprise that characterized the first quarter of the last century, development was working like yeast...

The sentence describes how New Orleans grew after the "purchase of the Louisiana territory" and how "development was working like yeast". Yeast multiplies rapidly, so the reader can conclude that New Orleans was growing rapidly.

Example 2

Read the following sentence. Draw a conclusion based upon the information presented.

> "A rosy-faced servant-maid opened the door, and smiled as she took the letter which he silently offered."

The reader can conclude, based on the sentence, that the servant-maid is friendly. The words "rosy-faced" and "smiled" lead the reader to this conclusion. People who are friendly are often described as having rosy complexions and smiling as a common sign of pleasantness. The reader can also assume, from the sentence, that the letter does not present any threat or unpleasantness to the servant-maid. The person presenting the letter does not have anything to say upon offering it, so perhaps he is waiting to see how the servant-maid will react.

When interpreting a sentence, always look for key words that describe a character. The author carefully crafts a description of each character, to form a picture in the reader's mind about what the character is like.

Recognize Irrelevant Evidence

Claims are sometimes introduced that use evidence which is not relevant to the subject of the text. It may be because the evidence does not come from a credible source, or because the evidence may have little to do with the claim. When evaluating evidence, ask yourself what relationship the evidence has to a claim. For instance, if a writer says that global warming is not occurring and then cites evidence from a study that is 25 years old, it is probably outdated and irrelevant to the claim. The reader should be aware of this possibility and disregard any irrelevant evidence. The reader should also be wary of any evidence that is not from a valid source.

Synthesizing Information

Synthesizing a Text with Existing Knowledge

Synthesizing is similar to summarizing but it takes it one step further. Synthesizing involves taking the main points of a text and comparing it with existing knowledge to create a new idea, perspective, or way of thinking.

Another term for knowledge that you already have is **schema**. The plural form of this word is **schemata**. Schemata contain all the ideas you have about something. Synthesizing is all about how schemata change over time with the introduction of new information.

EXAMPLE

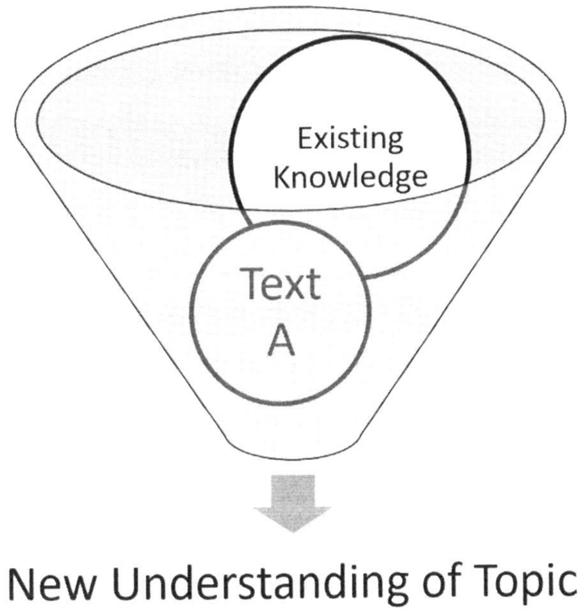

Using self-questioning strategies can help readers synthesize texts with their schemata to increase or change their understanding of topics. These questions include

- What do I already know about this topic?
- Is any of this new information?
- Has my perspective changed now that I've read this?
- What do I understand now that I didn't before?
- What are the main ideas of this text?
- How do the parts of the text fit together to create meaning?
- Are there any text-to-text, text-to-self, or text-to-world connections here?

SYNTHESIZING TEXTS WITHOUT EXISTING KNOWLEDGE

If the reader is completely unfamiliar with the topic, they will have no background knowledge. In this case, instead of using existing knowledge, synthesizing may instead be done by combining the ideas provided in two or three different texts. The reader must make connections between the texts, determine how the ideas fit together, and gather evidence to support the new perspective.

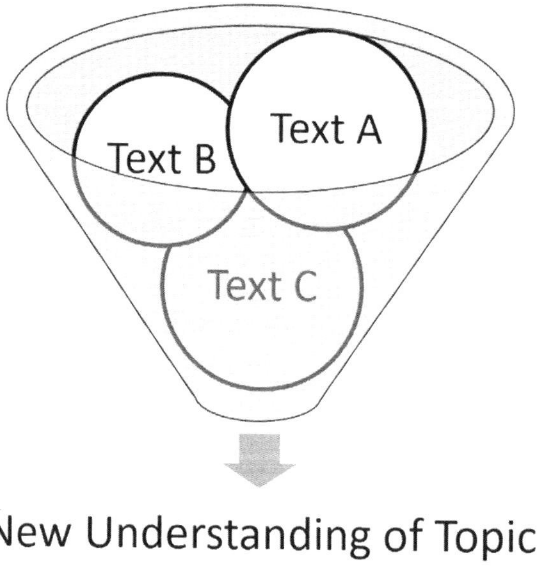

Using self-questioning strategies can help readers synthesize texts to increase their understanding of topics. In this case, readers are creating new schemata as they read. These questions include

- What do these texts have in common?
- What is different between these texts?
- What new information have I learned?
- What do I understand now that I didn't before?
- How do these texts relate to one another?
- If I think of these texts as parts of one whole, what meaning do they create together?
- What predictions can I make about this topic?

Literary Elements in Poetry

Meter, Rhyme, and Repetitions of Sounds

The **meter** of a poem refers to the number of syllables per line as well as the pattern of emphasis on those syllables. The use of meter gives a poem a rhythmic context and contributes to the poem's flow. Certain types of meter can also make a poem more appealing to the reader or represent natural speech rhythms.

Rhymes repeat the ending sound of words: "So very soon/We will fly to the moon." Here the "oo" sound is repeated in the words *soon* and *moon*. Rhymes are frequently used in poetry, mostly older forms of poetry rather than modern poems.

Another type of repetition is **alliteration**. Alliteration repeats beginning sounds, usually consonants: "Rah, rah, rah," the crowd cried, "rah, rah, rah." It is often used in poetry as well as in spoken forms of writing.

Rhyme Scheme

When determining what a poem's rhyme scheme is, readers should look at the last word of each line to see which words rhyme with each other. Words that rhyme are assigned a letter of the alphabet, beginning with "a." The next time words rhyme, if the rhyme is different than the last one, they assigned a new letter, going forward in order of the alphabet until the poem is over or there are no more rhymes. This sounds complicated, but it's easy with practice.

Let's take a look at an excerpt from Dylan Thomas' poem "Do not go gentle into that good night":

> Do not go gentle into that good night,
> Old age should burn and rave at close of day;
> Rage, rage against the dying of the light.
>
> Though wise men at their end know dark is right,
> Because their words had forked no lightning they
> Do not go gentle into that good night.

The words at the end of the lines are *night, day, light, right, they,* and *night.*

We know that the first rhyme is assigned the letter "a," and can clearly see that *night, light,* and *right* all rhyme, so we can mark the poem like this

Do not go gentle into that good night,	**a**	
Old age should burn and rave at close of day;		
Rage, rage against the dying of the light.		**a**
Though wise men at their end know dark is right,		**a**
Because their words had forked no lightning they		
Do not go gentle into that good night.	**a**	

Now, we'll look at the only other rhyme in the poem, which is made up of the words *day* and *they.* This rhyme does not rhyme with the first set of words, so it gets a new letter, "b."

Do not go gentle into that good night,	**a**	
Old age should burn and rave at close of day;	**b**	
Rage, rage against the dying of the light.		**a**
Though wise men at their end know dark is right,		**a**
Because their words had forked no lightning they	**b**	
Do not go gentle into that good night.	**a**	

After looking at all six lines and determining how they rhyme, we can confidently say that the rhyme scheme for this excerpt is a, b, a, a, b, a.

Rhymes are used at the discretion of the poet and are not always mandatory. Many modern poems—actually, most of them—use a blank verse, where there are no rhyme schemes. However, there are many formal poetic types, such as the sonnet, that have a specific rhyme scheme that poets must follow to achieve that kind of poetic form.

Example

Explain the rhyme scheme of the following excerpt from a poem entitled "Alone" by Edgar Allan Poe.

> From childhood's hour I have not been
> As others were; I have not seen
> As others saw; I could not bring
> My passions from a common spring.
> From the same source I have not taken
> My sorrow; I could not awaken
> My heart to joy at the same tone;
> And all I loved, I loved alone.

The rhyme scheme that Edgar Allan Poe uses in this excerpt from his poem "Alone" is: a, a, b, b, c, c, d, d, e, e. Every two lines rhyme, but the rhyme is not repeated in the other lines. This is a rather unusual rhyme scheme; many others have lines that repeat the rhyme scheme, but not in a consecutive order, such as a, b, a, b or a, b, c a, b, c.

Graphical Elements in Poem

Graphic elements in a poem such as capitalization, line length, and word position can call special attention to words or phrases. Capitalization can signal the beginning of a sentence, or all caps may be used to provide emphasis. Line length can be used to help create a shape, like in concrete poems, or to create a bold statement, like a one-word line. A poet can create tension by using line length and punctuation independently of one another. Word position can be used to contribute to a feeling, or it can also be used to help create a shape, so poets are often careful where they end lines.

Poetic Form Contributes to Meaning

The form or structure of a poem is extremely important to the meaning of the text. Poetry comes out of guidelines that were developed in Europe and England and then were brought to the United States, where they were used and sometimes changed to serve a different purpose. For example, strict rhyming poetry has given way to blank verse, and the choice of the structure of the poem or play can give the reader a hint as to its meaning.

Epic Poetry and Lyric Poetry

An **epic poem** is a lengthy, narrative poem that usually tells a story about a serious or heroic deed. These types of poems are important within specific cultures or groups of people. In an epic, the hero tends to go on a journey or a quest. The hero meets many adversaries and enemies along the way. Through each encounter the hero may learn something new. When the hero returns home, he has changed significantly through his journey. Most often the hero's trials are related to morals that were important to the specific culture.

Lyric poetry is a type of poetry that expresses the author's personal feelings. This type of poetry is almost always emotional. They author will use sensory language to influence the audience's emotions. Originally, lyric poetry was written to be sung along with a lyre, a type of stringed instrument. It is a type of poetry that doesn't have to rhyme or even be set to music.

Organization of Informational Texts

Introducing a Topic

When writing an informational or explanatory text, the author will need to introduce the topic that the text will be about. There are numerous strategies that can help improve the reader's comprehension of the subject. An author may choose to define key words that a reader may not be familiar with, classify information or compare and contrast it, or use a cause and effect relationship in the report. Charts and tables are extremely useful for displaying complicated information and the use of headings can help signify where certain information will be found. Multimedia devices, including video and audio, can also improve the way in which an author displays his material because they are appealing to the audience or reader.

Developing a Topic

To develop a topic in an informational or explanatory text, an author needs to use relevant facts that support details related to the main topic. The topic may be included in a topic sentence or opening statement and then followed by supporting details. Some of the supporting details should be concrete facts that have been researched and confirmed. Quotations of experts in the field of the topic are another good source for supporting material. Quoting experts gives variety and credence to a text. Examples, charts, and multimedia techniques can also be used to enhance the presentation, but these extras should not be used as a substitute for solid supporting details.

Example

Analyze the beginning of this informational text and tell what could be added to improve it.

> The journey of the salmon from salt water to fresh water to breed is one of the wonders of nature. This journey, called the salmon run, is difficult because the fish must swim upriver against the current. Some even leap up waterfalls as they make their way back to their original breeding grounds.

This seems like a good start to an informational text. The first sentence establishes the topic. It tells what the report is going to be about. It also includes two supporting details to tell more about the topic. This is one way to introduce and develop a topic in a report or other informational or explanatory text. What should come next are more supporting details and also sources for the information that is cited; a quotation from an authority of the salmon run would make the report stronger and give it credence. Some statistics, facts, figures about how many salmon make the run each year and how many survive would also be of interest.

Using Appropriate Transitions

When writing an informational or explanatory text it is important to use appropriate transitions that will clarify the relationships among ideas and concepts. For example, to show causality between ideas, use transition words or phrases, such as "therefore," "consequently," and "as a result of." To show comparison or contrast relationships, words such as "however," "on the other hand," "but," "in contrast," and "similarly" should be used. Transition words and expressions to introduce examples include "for example, "for instance," "namely" and "that is." The order of importance can also be shown through transitions, such as "at first," "former," "latter," "primarily" and "second."

Importance of Using Precise Language and Domain-Specific Vocabulary

When writing informational or explanatory texts it is of utmost importance to use precise language and domain-specific vocabulary to explain your main idea and supporting details. Generalized vocabulary will not help the audience grasp the points that you are attempting to make because they will not accurately reflect your main idea and supporting details. Domain-specific vocabulary is important to use because it will accurately describe or explain the ideas or processes that are central to your text. When you research a subject, make sure to familiarize yourself with any vocabulary that is involved in its explanation. Use context clues, dictionaries, or, if necessary, a technical dictionary to decode any words that you are not familiar with. Also include definitions of domain-specific vocabulary in your text to enlighten readers.

Establishing and Maintaining a Formal Style

When writing an informational or explanatory text it is important to establish and maintain a formal style of writing. Do not use a colloquial or casual tone. It is necessary to use the third person and to make the sentences longer and more complex. It is also important not to use contractions when you write. A formal style announces that the writer is serious about his or her subject and wants to write an objective paper. This can be done by keeping the main ideas and supporting details clear, to the point, but as complex as they need to be. A formal style also means that the writer will not include a personal opinion that is not justified.

Example

Discuss why the following excerpt is an example of formal writing.

> Richard Spruce found his life's work in the jungles of South America. Spruce grew up in a part of England that was filled with plants growing wild and free. His love of plants developed early. When he read a book about the Amazon jungle in Brazil, he decided to go there to study the area's plant life.

This is a good example of formal writing. It is objective and unbiased. The author uses the third person perspective, which formal writing is supposed to do. He sets out his main idea in the initial topic sentence, and then gives good supporting details. His sentences are somewhat complex and varied. He does not use any contractions, which are not used in formal writing, and the language is not colloquial or casual. The style of writing matches the subject. At the same time, the writing is not dull; the reader is intrigued and wants to learn more. Formal writing does not have to be uninteresting.

Importance of a Concluding Statement

A concluding statement or section that follows from and supports the information or explanation is important to a text because the conclusion helps to focus the important points in a text and also provides closure to the reader or audience. A good conclusion attempts to sum up the passage and any conclusions that the author makes so that the audience feels they have received a logical ending to the text. An effective conclusion gives the passage the weight it needs to have an effect. The conclusion should not make the reader feel that there is more information to follow, but rather set the tone for the ending of the topic.

Techniques Used by Authors

There are various techniques that authors use to make connections among and distinctions between individuals, ideas, or events. An author may choose to compare and contrast individuals, ideas, or events. This allows the reader to quickly see how something or someone is similar to or different from another thing or person. A second technique is through the use of analogies. An author may liken an idea, individual, or events by using analogies to show how they are similar and make her point clearer. An author might also put individuals, ideas, or events into categories to show how they are linked.

Example

Read the excerpt and tell how the author makes connections between ideas.

> On the exterior it looked tidy and pleasant—a little log cabin with a fence around it. The lawn was cut close and the bushes were all tended to. No weeds in this yard. Inside was another story. The furniture was covered with dust. Huge spider webs dangled from the ceiling, and the floor was covered with dirt.

The author is comparing and contrasting the outside of a cabin with the inside. This is how the ideas are connected. Although the exterior looked tidy and pleasant, the interior was completely the opposite. It was dusty and dirty and had not been cleaned in a long time. Writers often link ideas. When a compare-and-contrast connection is made, the reader is quick to see the similarities and the differences between the two ideas or people being compared. Other ways to connect ideas is through categorizing. This technique is often used in scientific texts. Analogy is another way to connect ideas. This shows the relationship between two things or people so it is clearer to a reader.

Analyzing the Structure of a Paragraph

When reading a paragraph, a close study of the way in which is it structured is helpful. The reader should first look to see how the author begins the paragraph. Does she open the paragraph with a topic sentence or does she use some other technique, such as a humorous or dramatic statement, to begin the paragraph? If the second is true, does a topic sentence follow or do supporting details come next? If the topic sentence is at the start of the paragraph, supporting details would follow it. The last sentence is the conclusion. Some conclusions can be topic sentences, but that is not usual. The last sentence most often brings closure to the paragraph and signals the end. Paragraphs can also have an overall structure.

Organizing Ideas

There are many ways to present information so that it is easier to understand. One effective tool is headings. Each heading introduces a new concept or idea in a text and allows the reader to see, just by skimming, what the article is about and which points are being covered. Another useful tool is graphics. Graphics are extremely useful because they present a lot of detailed information in a visual form that is easy to understand. Instead of putting the information in a paragraph where it can be lost to the reader, it can be put into a graphic such as a chart or table that will make it much more approachable. Multimedia such as voice-over, videos or even movies are other excellent ways to present information; in this modern world, people respond very easily to this kind of presentation. Difficult material can be made much more enjoyable through the use of these tools.

Organizational Patterns

When writing there are a variety of ways that an author can choose to organize their text. It is important for them to choose the pattern that best presents their information, as not all patterns will work for every piece of writing. Some examples are

Advantage/Disadvantage

The author chooses a topic or concept and addresses both the advantages and disadvantages (or pros and cons) of the subject. In this type of text the author is not trying to persuade their audience to choose a side, but rather, to inform the reader of all the possible positive and negative effects.

Cause and Effect

The author will write about relationship between two events that occur, where the second event occurs as a result of the first.

For example, a text may discuss a school policy stating that when a student is late to school too many times, they receive a detention. Later in the text, we might see a student repeatedly arriving late to school, after which he is given a detention. In this example, the **cause** is the student being late to school, and the **effect** is the student receiving a detention.

Classification

The author chooses a topic and divides it into smaller parts or groups in order to discuss them individually. These types of texts address how parts work within a whole, or what characteristics can be used to classify a given subject or concept.

Chronological Order

The author organizes the progression of events based upon when they occurred and what was included in each step of the story. By organizing the text in this way the author presents all necessary information about the six questions readers can ask to help themselves understand the text: who, what, when, where, why, and how.

Compare and Contrast

The author will show similarities and differences between items or events.

For example, the author may write about cats and dogs. They might start by giving a brief description of the two. Then they will want to point out all of the similarities, such as; they both have tails, and both are kept as pets. Next, they will explain the differences, such as; dogs are canines, while cats are felines. They will try to provide as much detail as possible about both the similarities and the differences.

Definition

Authors introduce a concept or word and then explain or describe it. This type of text often included examples that will help the reader gain understanding of what is presumably a new concept for them.

Inductive / Deductive

Authors organize ideas from general to specific or specific to general. If ideas are organized **inductively**, they are arranged from specific facts to general conclusions. If ideas are organized from general conclusions to specific facts, they are organized **deductively**. A reader can make a logical assumption about a topic based on the facts that are presented in the text.

For example, in these two sentences the ideas are organized deductively, from general to specific.

> Many canoers use the lake in the summer. Jeff learned how to canoe last summer, and is on his way to the lake now.

The idea that "Many canoers use the lake in the summer" is a general idea. The facts that Jeff already knows how to canoe and is headed to the lake are specific to him as a character.

Order of Importance

The author puts the information in the text in order of what is most important. Order of importance can be either increasing or decreasing, depending on how the writer wants to structure the work.

Proposition and Support

The author states a proposition that they believe to be true, and then provides support for that proposition in the paper. The topics that use this type of structure are generally things that reader might feel uncertain about or might not already have an opinion about. The support that the author gives for the proposition should include facts, statistics, logic, and reasoning. The more hard evidence an author can give the reader, the better it will help convince them to see things from the author's point of view.

IDENTIFYING ORGANIZATIONAL STRATEGIES

EXAMPLE 1

Explain which organization pattern would be the best choice for this writer and why.

> Sara is writing a report on sea turtles. She has researched the various dangers that they face: their predators, the difficulties they encounter in their life cycle starting with their birth, their migration to the ocean, and the dangers that await them as they mature. She is unsure of how to organize her report.

A cause and effect order would seem to be the best idea for Sara because she would be able to identify the causes and effects of the dangers that sea turtles encounter. She could organize the report so that each paragraph deals with a different threat, using headings to identify what would be in each section. A chart would also be useful because it puts the same information in a clear format so that readers would be able to refer to it. She might also consider using a video showing baby turtles migrating towards the open sea, which would give her audience an even greater understanding of the turtles' plight.

EXAMPLE 2

Identify the text structure that is used in the following sentences:

> Madison and her brother Jake used to live on a wind-torn island in the Chesapeake Bay. Last year they moved to Baltimore, a city in Maryland. Next summer they plan to visit the island where they grew up.

Chronological order is used as a text structure in the example sentences, as they are organized according to the passage of time. Note that each sentence refers to a point in time. The first sentence refers to where the siblings lived in the past. The second sentence refers to the siblings' move to Baltimore last year. The final sentence refers to what the siblings plan to do in the future. By referring to a specific place in time, the reader can see what occurred in the story during that time period. An author will often use flashback to indicate what happened in the past, and foreshadowing to give the reader a glimpse of what may occur in the future.

EXAMPLE 3

Identify the text structure that is used in the following sentences:

> Three cousins lived in the same small town. One day the cousins decided to journey together to enter a singing contest across the country. The cousins won the contest and made their hometown fans proud.

The information in the story can be organized according to the passage of time, called chronological order. The story will start based in the cousins' hometown, to give some background on where the cousins come from. Subsequent events in the story will occur over time based on the cousins' motivations due to their background. The story will end by referring back to how far the cousins have come from their small-town roots.

Example 4

Read the following thesis statement and discuss the organizational pattern the author will use:

> While many people are content with the DVD players they already have at home, Blu-ray technology provides for better viewing of high definition video.

From this thesis statement the reader can assume that the author is going to use a deductive presentation of ideas. The author starts with the conclusion that Blu-ray technology is a better method for watching high definition video than DVD. The reader can assume that in the rest of the text, the author will discuss the reasons why he arrived at this conclusion, most likely providing details and examples that will support his conclusion. When the conclusion is presented first, then followed by specific examples, the ideas are presented in deductive order.

Example 5

Read the following thesis statement and discuss the organizational pattern that the author will use:

> Throughout his life, Thomas Edison used his questioning and creative mind to become one of America's greatest inventors.

Based on the thesis statement, the reader can assume that the author is going to use chronological order to organize the information in the rest of the essay. The words "throughout his life" clue the reader in to the chronological organizational structure, which presents information in the order than it occurred. The author will probably discuss Edison's childhood and initial inventions first and then move on to his later queries and inventions. Chronological order is often used as the organizational structure in biographies as a way to logically present the important events in a person's life.

Author's Purpose and Message

Author's Purpose

The purpose of a text is the author's main reason for writing the text. As the reader reads a text, they should always try to figure out the author's purpose for writing as this will help them to better understand the message that the author is trying to convey.

Informational Texts

- Inform the reader on a topic that they previously knew nothing about, such as many non-fiction texts.
- The author will usually include sources of information for an informative piece.
- For example, an informative paper on early Native American Indian tribes would detail where Native American Indians lived, what types of foods they ate, how they bartered for goods, and other aspects of their culture.

Persuasive Texts

- Influence the reader to think a certain way about a topic, calling them to action or pointing them toward resources that would help them to learn more about the topic.
- A Proposition and Support paper would be an example of this, where an author gives their opinion and then tries to convince the reader to see something from their point of view.
- An author will often use positive expert testimonials when trying to persuade the reader to accept a given point-of-view.

- For example, an author may try to persuade the reader that technology is negatively affecting social interaction, and that limits should be set on how much people can use their technological devices.

EXPRESSIVE TEXTS

- Express the author or speaker's opinion or emotions about a topic. Generally, expressive texts include descriptive words to clearly show the reader how the author or speaker feels.
- For example, the author may think that history is important for all people to study, and express the opinion that education without history class would be incomplete.

ENTERTAINING TEXTS

- Entertain the reader, such as in most fictional texts.
- For example, Lois Lowry, the author of *The Giver,* entertains his readers with the story of a young boy named Jonas who is learning how to navigate his unexpected life assignment.

Review Video: Understanding the Author's Intent
Visit mometrix.com/academy and enter code: 511819

DETERMINING THE PURPOSE OF A TEXT

While reading a text, you should always try to determine its purpose. To do so, ask yourself why the author wrote the text and what affect the writing has on you. Is the purpose to explain something or tell how to do something? Does the text try to persuade you of something? Perhaps the text is making an appeal to your emotions. The signs that a text is attempting to persuade you include an author offering an opinion and telling why she thinks that way. On the other hand, if a text is simply

informative, it will have many facts that will give details about an event or person or a thing, but not try to persuade you of anything. Manuals that come with equipment are clearly not persuasive; they simply are instructive.

During the writing process, the author may decide to **change the purpose of the text**. When this occurs, the entire story is changed. For example, an author may write a story to inform the reader about a given topic, such as the need to stay hydrated during hot weather. If the author decides to change the purpose of the text to persuade the reader to drink a particular type of sports beverage to stay hydrated during hot weather, the text becomes an advertisement. While the original purpose of the text was to inform, the new purpose of the text is to persuade. Changing the purpose of a text can alter the length of the story, the type of words used (descriptive vs. sensational), and the amount of information included. You may be asked to identify the overall purpose of an entire text, or the purpose of a sentence or paragraph within that text.

EXAMPLE 1

Read the following sentence. State the author's point in writing the sentence, whether it is to inform, entertain, persuade, or state an opinion.

> Bristlecone pines are remarkable. They are the longest-lived form of plant life in the world. These trees can live as long as 5,000 years. Some bristlecone pines standing today in the western United States were seedlings when the Egyptian pyramids were being built. They were mature trees by the year 1 AD.

The purpose of the excerpt is to inform. The way in which a reader can tell this is that the text has concrete facts and details about the bristlecone pines. It does not have any opinions, other than the obvious one, that "bristlecone pines are remarkable." The author of the excerpt is not trying to persuade the reader of anything other than that. And the details that she includes make the pines very remarkable. The formal language is to the point and the information is interesting. The writer wants people to learn about the bristlecone pines; she is not selling them nor is she asking people to protect them.

Example 2

Read the following excerpt from *The Diary of a Young Girl* by Anne Frank. State the author's point in writing the excerpt, whether it is to inform, entertain, persuade, or state an opinion.

> It's really a wonder that I haven't dropped all my ideals, because they seem so absurd and impossible to carry out. Yet I keep them, because in spite of everything, I still believe that people are really good at heart.

The excerpt shown here is stating an opinion, so it would be considered an expressive text excerpt. The author is describing her feelings and her belief that people are inherently good, despite everything that has happened to her. The author does not try to convince the reader to believe the same thing, nor does she try to inform by providing factual information.

Example 3

Read the following sentence. State the author's point in writing the sentence, whether it is to inform, entertain, persuade, or state an opinion.

> Softsuds is the best shampoo on the market. It will leave your hair tangle-free and shiny. Try it out to see for yourself. Pick some up today!

The sentences shown here contains persuasive language about a certain brand of shampoo, which might be used in a commercial or other advertisement. The author is not trying to give factual information about the shampoo. He is not trying to describe the aroma or feeling of the shampoo's lather. The author is not telling a story about an experience using the shampoo either. Thus, from this deduction, one can determine that the author is writing with the purpose of influencing or persuading the reader to use the Softsuds brand of shampoo.

Author's Perspective

The author will always have specific ideas about a story before they draw up a plot line. The author will know what events they want to take place, how they want the characters to interact, and how the story will resolve. An author will also have an opinion on the topic, or series of events, which is presented in the story, based on their own prior experience and beliefs.

Each story can be taken in whatever direction the author wishes. A story will often make sense based on societal norms, but the author can purposely choose to go against these norms to shock the reader. For example, if an author wrote a story about a man who enjoyed living in the bayous of Louisiana, the audience would not expect the character to promptly move to Alaska. Sometimes an author will put a twist in a story just to surprise the reader.

Example 4

Read the following excerpt:

> Dear Editor: We must support the "Save-the-Buffalo" bill before Congress. Anyone with any concern about animal life and the environment must support this bill. The people who vote against it are selfish fools who don't care about the environment.

Describe the perspective of the author and tell if the letter could be improved.

> The perspective of the author of the letter is clear; he states what he thinks right away. He is in favor of the "Save-the-Buffalo" bill and he argues that people should support it if they care about the environment. He also insults those who are against by the bill by calling them selfish fools and saying they don't care about the environment. This letter is not subtle in any way. It is the complete opposite. The letter could be improved by the author using facts or figures to back up his argument rather than insulting those who do not agree with him.

Author's Use of Print and Graphic Features

Print and Graphic Features

An author may show information in a chart, a graph, in paragraph format, or as a list. Information may also be shown in a picture or a diagram. The way an author chooses to show information is often based on the purpose of the text and the audience that the text is meant to reach.

A reader may be asked to answer questions based on the graphic by itself, how the graphic relates to the text, or how the text would best be shown in a graphic form.

Cause and Effect Graphic Organizers

Often used to map the **elements of a story**. A reader might read a story about a string of events and then be asked to correctly fill in either the **cause** or **effect** of an event in the story.

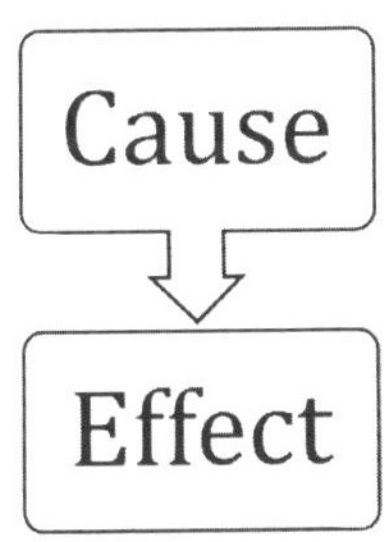

Review Video: Graphic Organizers
Visit mometrix.com/academy and enter code: 665513

Example

Read the following excerpt from *Holes* by Louis Sachar and decide what effect Stanley's letter has on his mother:

> Dear Stanley,
> It was wonderful to hear from you. Your letter made me feel like one of the other moms who can afford to send their kids to summer camp. I know it's not the same, but I am very proud of you for trying to make the best of a bad situation.

A **cause and effect** graphic organizer for this excerpt might look something like this:

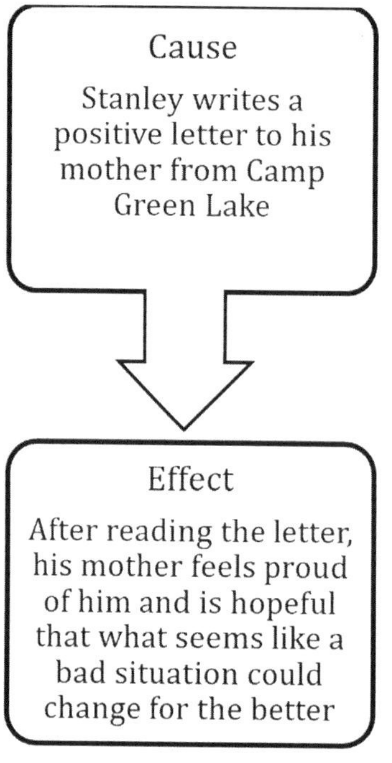

LINE GRAPHS

Used for measuring general **trends over time**. For example, this line graph shows an overall upward trend in the amount of candy bars sold for four weeks.

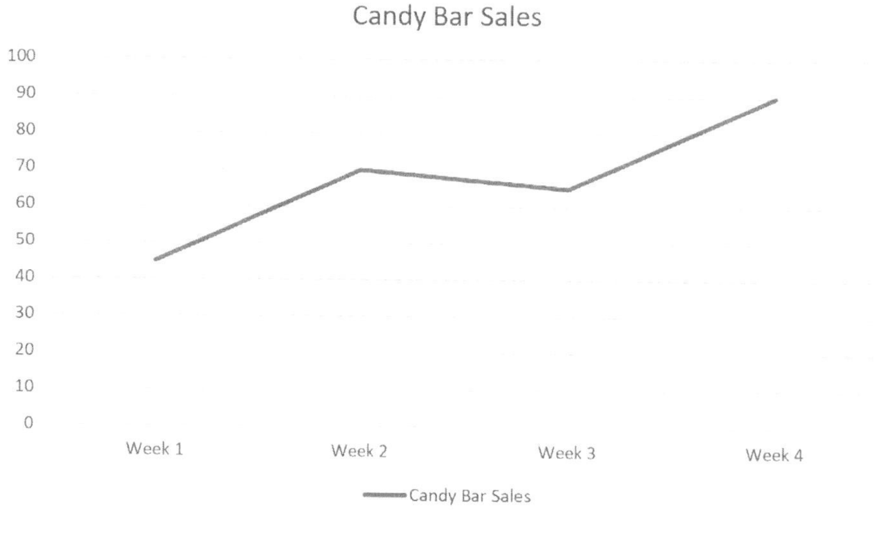

Circle Graphs (Also Called Pie Charts)

Used to represent information that can be shown as **parts of a whole**. For example, this graph shows the results of people being asked about their favorite color:

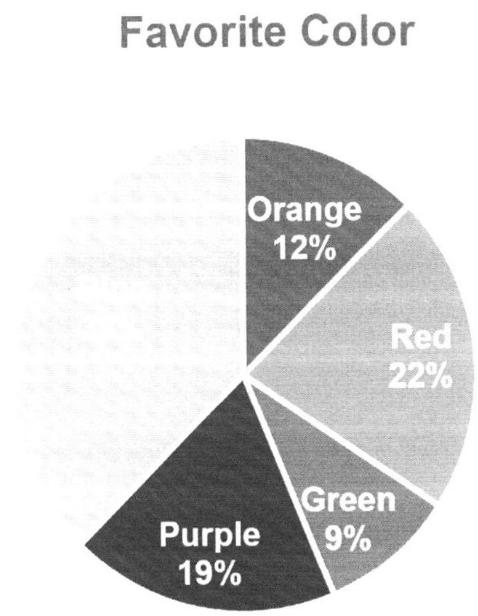

Bar Graphs

Used to illustrate sets of numerical data. The bar graph is one of the most common visual representations of information. For example, this graph is a different way of representing the same results as those in the circle graph:

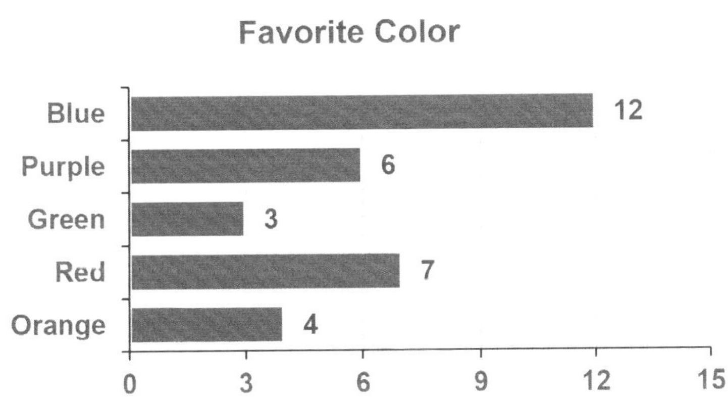

Illustrations and Photographs

Authors may choose to include **illustrations** or **photographs** (or both) with their texts. These two image types both show something from the text or give more information about the text.

- Illustrations are drawings of an object. They may be based on reality, or they may represent an artist's abstract idea. For example, this is an illustration of a 1903 automobile

- Photographs are pictures of objects. They are generally extremely realistic, and most often show an object as it actually existed at that moment in time. For example, this is a photograph of a 1917 automobile

Both illustrations and photographs give the reader another way to relate to and understand the text. The reader may be asked how the image relates to the text, what type of caption the image should be given, or why the author chose to include the image with the text.

Diagrams

Used to show information in a visual way. There are many different types of diagrams, including

- Diagrams that show the parts of an object, how they work together, or how they should be put together. This is an example of a diagram which shows how gears turn together

- Diagrams that show how information is related are called **Venn Diagrams**. These are ways to visually see the way in which two different ideas overlap. This is an example of a Venn Diagram comparing cats and dogs

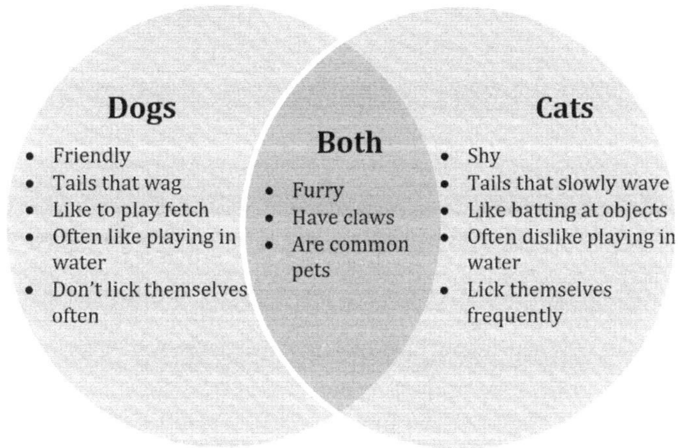

Author's Use of Figurative Language

Literal and Figurative Language

Many types of text use both **literal language**, which means just what it says, and **figurative language**, which allows the writer to expand the way in which he or she uses language. When an author uses figurative language, she connects things in an exaggerated and non-literal way in order to create a memorable image, which helps to describe a situation in a new way for the reader.

Review Video: Figurative Language
Visit mometrix.com/academy and enter code: 584902

Imagery

Imagery is the use of **descriptive language** to add life or feeling to a work of literature. Many authors add literary and sound devices to create vivid pictures in the minds of their readers. Most of the time, imagery is thought to be one of the best ways to help readers fully understand and remember a work.

The most common forms of imagery are those that appeal to the sense of sight and sound. Imagery that appeals to the sense of sight, or **visual imagery**, helps the reader picture an event in their mind, usually by including specific details in the text that are not strictly necessary for the purpose of the story, but allow the reader to more easily envision the scene. Some common forms of figurative language that help create visual imagery include.

Metaphor

- Puts one idea in place of another to draw a parallel between the two ideas.
- For example, an author might write "Her room was a pigsty," to compare a person's bedroom to a dirty spot where pigs sleep.

Simile

- Shows similarity between two ideas or objects, using the words "**like**" or "**as**"
- For example, an author might write "The princess is as beautiful as a rose" to compare the appearance of a woman to a beautiful flower.

Symbolism

- Using one object to stand for something else.
- For example, an author may include a flag flying high throughout a story to show pride in the characters' country and to represent the idea of patriotism.

Hyperbole

- An extreme exaggeration of an idea.
- For example, a character might say "I'm starving to death!" to show that they are really hungry. Most of the time a character who says this is not literally going to die from hunger, they are just ready for a snack.

Irony

- Uses sarcasm or humor (usually with an emphasis on the opposite) to show difference from literal meaning.
- For example, if a character says "Well today must be my lucky day!" after they left their homework on the kitchen table, they are being ironic. The irony used here helps show that it is definitely *not* the character's lucky day.

Personification

- Gives life or human characteristics to an inanimate object
- For example, if an author writes "The trees whispered to each other across the wide blue sky," they are using personification to help the reader imagine the scene. Trees are not human beings, so they do not whisper, but the image created in the reader stands out more than a literal description would.

Example 1

Discuss the kind of figurative language used by comedian Will Ferrell in this excerpt from his Harvard Commencement Address:

> I graduated from the University of Life, all right? I received a degree from the School of Hard Knocks. Our colors were black and blue, baby. I had office hours with the Dean of Bloody Noses, all right? I borrowed my class notes from Professor Knuckle Sandwich and his teaching assistant, Ms. Fat Lip Thanh Nguyen. That's the kind of school I went to for real, okay?

This excerpt is an example of an **extended metaphor**. While humorous in nature, Ferrell is comparing the idea of 'a formal education' to the idea of the 'real-world education' he received. These two ideas are unlike, and by placing them right next to one another for comparison, he highlights how different his experience was from the experiences of most of the graduates listening to him speak. This powerful metaphor serves his ultimate purpose of making sure the Harvard Class of 2003 recognized how lucky they were to be given so many educational opportunities.

Example 2

Discuss the kind of figurative language used in the following poem by the Scottish poet Robert Burns.

> O my luve's like a red, red rose
> That's newly sprung in June;
> O my luve's like the melodie
> That's sweetly played in tune.

The poet uses **similes** to create an image in this poem. The two similes here occur when the speaker says that his love is "**like** a red, red rose" and that she is also "**like** the melodie." These are examples of similes because they use the comparing word 'like' to compare two things. They are not metaphors because metaphors do not use the comparing words 'like' or 'as.' The poem paints an image of the speaker's love by comparing her to a red rose that has newly sprung and a melody that is sweetly played.

EXAMPLE 3

Read the following excerpt from "The Raven" by Edgar Allan Poe, identify the metaphor, and discuss how it impacts the text:

> And the raven, never flitting, still is sitting, still is sitting
> On the pallid bust of Pallas just above my chamber door;
> And his eyes have all the seeming of a demon's that is dreaming

One **metaphor** in the excerpt from "The Raven" by Edgar Allan Poe is: 'And his eyes have all the seeming of a demon's that is dreaming' The metaphor compares the raven's eyes with a demon, which shows that the speaker thinks there is evil in the bird. This helps contribute to the overall tone of the poem and the reader's understanding of how the speaker views the bird.

EXAMPLE 5

Read the excerpt written by Martin Luther King, Jr. and identify the type of figurative language Dr. King is using.

> One hundred years later, the Negro is still languishing in the corners of American society and finds himself an exile in his own land.

In this excerpt, Dr. King uses a strong **metaphor** to express what he feels when he compares 'the Negro' to 'an exile in his own land'. An exile is someone who is cast out, but in this case, he is referring to a person living in his own land, so this is an extremely emotional and effective way of demonstrating the problems that African Americans were facing at this time. Figurative language is an effective way to get a point across, as in the case of this metaphor.

Reading Practice Test #1

Questions 1 -12 pertain to the following passages:

***Call of the Wild* by Jack London**

Buck did not read the newspapers, or he would have known that trouble was brewing, not alone for himself, but for every tide-water dog, strong of muscle and with warm, long hair, from Puget Sound to San Diego. Because men, groping in the Arctic darkness, had found a yellow metal, and because steamship and transportation companies were booming the find, thousands of men were rushing into the Northland. These men wanted dogs, and the dogs they wanted were heavy dogs, with strong muscles by which to toil, and furry coats to protect them from the frost.

Buck lived at a big house in the sun-kissed Santa Clara Valley. Judge Miller's place, it was called. It stood back from the road, half hidden among the trees, through which glimpses could be caught of the wide cool veranda that ran around its four sides. The house was approached by gravelled driveways which wound about through wide-spreading lawns and under the interlacing boughs of tall poplars. At the rear things were on even a more spacious scale than at the front. There were great stables, where a dozen grooms and boys held forth, rows of vine-clad servants' cottages, an endless and orderly array of outhouses, long grape arbors, green pastures, orchards, and berry patches. Then there was the pumping plant for the artesian well, and the big cement tank where Judge Miller's boys took their morning plunge and kept cool in the hot afternoon.

And over this great demesne Buck ruled. Here he was born, and here he had lived the four years of his life. It was true, there were other dogs, there could not but be other dogs on so vast a place, but they did not count. They came and went, resided in the populous kennels, or lived obscurely in the recesses of the house after the fashion of Toots, the Japanese pug, or Ysabel, the Mexican hairless,—strange creatures that rarely put nose out of doors or set foot to ground. On the other hand, there were the fox terriers, a score of them at least, who yelped fearful promises at Toots and Ysabel looking out of the windows at them and protected by a legion of housemaids armed with brooms and mops.

But Buck was neither house-dog nor kennel-dog. The whole realm was his. He plunged into the swimming tank or went hunting with the Judge's sons; he escorted Mollie and Alice, the Judge's daughters, on long twilight or early morning rambles; on wintry nights he lay at the Judge's feet before the roaring library fire; he carried the Judge's grandsons on his back, or rolled them in the grass, and guarded their footsteps through wild adventures down to the fountain in the stable yard, and even beyond, where the paddocks were, and the berry patches. Among the terriers he stalked imperiously, and Toots and Ysabel he utterly ignored, for he was king,—king over all creeping, crawling, flying things of Judge Miller's place, humans included.

His father, Elmo, a huge St. Bernard, had been the Judge's inseparable companion, and Buck bid fair to follow in the way of his father. He was not so large,—he weighed only one hundred and forty pounds,—for his mother, Shep, had been a Scotch shepherd dog. Nevertheless, one hundred and forty pounds, to which was added the dignity that comes of good living and universal respect, enabled him to carry himself in right royal fashion.

During the four years since his puppyhood he had lived the life of a sated aristocrat; he had a fine pride in himself, was even a trifle egotistical, as country gentlemen sometimes become because of their insular situation. But he had saved himself by not becoming a mere pampered house-dog. Hunting and kindred outdoor delights had kept down the fat and hardened his muscles; and to him, as to the cold-tubbing races, the love of water had been a tonic and a health preserver.

And this was the manner of dog Buck was in the fall of 1897, when the Klondike strike dragged men from all the world into the frozen North. But Buck did not read the newspapers, and he did not know that Manuel, one of the gardener's helpers, was an undesirable acquaintance. Manuel had one besetting sin. He loved to play Chinese lottery. Also, in his gambling, he had one besetting weakness—faith in a system; and this made his damnation certain. For to play a system requires money, while the wages of a gardener's helper do not lap over the needs of a wife and numerous progenies.

The Judge was at a meeting of the Raisin Growers' Association, and the boys were busy organizing an athletic club, on the memorable night of Manuel's treachery. No one saw him and Buck go off through the orchard on what Buck imagined was merely a stroll. And with the exception of a solitary man, no one saw them arrive at the little flag station known as College Park. This man talked with Manuel, and money chinked between them.

1. What is the purpose of paragraphs 2-5?

a. To introduce all of the story's characters
b. To show Buck's personality
c. To introduce Buck
d. To show Buck's affection for Toots and Ysabel

2. Which sentence or phrase shows Buck's attitude about Judge Miller's place?

a. They came and went, resided in the populous kennels, or lived obscurely in the recesses of the house
b. The whole realm was his
c. He had a fine pride in himself
d. And to him, as to the cold-tubbing races, the love of water had been a tonic and a health preserver

3. The author uses the detail in paragraph 1 to

a. Describe Buck's life
b. Foreshadow Buck's story
c. Describe the story's setting
d. Introduce the story's villain

4. What is the significance of the Klondike strike in 1897?

a. It will lead to changes in Buck's life
b. It will cause more dogs to move to Judge Miller's place
c. It changed Elmo's life
d. It caused the Raisin Growers' Association to meet more frequently

5. The use of the word *imperiously* in paragraph four helps the reader know that Buck feels

a. Scared
b. Angry
c. Happy
d. Regal

6. The author organizes this selection mainly by

a. Describing Buck's life in the order in which it happened
b. Outlining Buck's history
c. Showing Buck's life and then showing a moment of change
d. Comparing Buck's life at Judge Miller's place to what came afterwards

7. Which answer choice best describes the purpose of the selection?

a. To set up a story by providing background information
b. To show Buck in a moment of heroism
c. To give details about the Klondike strike
d. To introduce all the dogs that live at Judge Miller's

8. In the future, Buck will probably

a. Continue to act like the king of Judge Miller's place
b. Reunite with his father, Elmo, and his mother, Shep
c. Leave Judge Miller's place against his will
d. Spend more time in the garden

9. This selection is part of a longer work. Based on the selection, what might be a theme of the larger work?

a. Change
b. Family
c. Hard work
d. Relationships

10. Paragraph 2 is mostly about:

a. The Santa Clara Valley
b. Judge Miller's place
c. Buck's lifestyle
d. The Klondike strike

11. Which sentence from the passage foreshadows the rest of the story?

a. And over this great demesne Buck ruled
b. These men wanted dogs, and the dogs they wanted were heavy dogs, with strong muscles by which to toil, and furry coats to protect them from the frost
c. His father, Elmo, a huge St. Bernard, had been the Judge's inseparable companion and Buck bid fair to follow in the way of his father
d. But he had saved himself by not becoming a mere pampered house-dog

12. What's the most logical explanation why Buck doesn't read the newspapers?

a. He's not interested in current events
b. He's busy exploring Judge Miller's place
c. The Raisin Growers' Association takes all his time
d. He's a dog

Questions 13 – 16 pertain to the following passage:

Andy Grant's Pluck by Horatio Alger

(1) The house and everything about it seemed just as it did when he left at the beginning of the school term. But Andy looked at them with different eyes.

(2) Then he had been in good spirits, eager to return to his school work.

Now something had happened, he did not yet know what.

(3) Mrs. Grant was in the back part of the house, and Andy was in the sitting room before she was fully aware of his presence. Then she came in from the kitchen, where she was preparing supper.

(4) Her face seemed careworn, but there was a smile upon it as she greeted her son.

(5) "Then you got my telegram?" she said. "I didn't think you would be here so soon."

(6) "I started at once, mother, for I felt anxious. What has happened? Are you all well?"

(7) "Yes, thank God, we are in fair health, but we have met with misfortune."

(8) "What is it?"

(9) "Nathan Lawrence, cashier of the bank in Benton, has disappeared with twenty thousand dollars of the bank's money."

(10) "What has that to do with father? He hasn't much money in that bank."

(11) "Your father is on Mr. Lawrence's bond to the amount of six thousand dollars."

(12) "I see," answered Andy, gravely, "How much will he lose?"

(13) "The whole of it."

(14) This, then, was what had happened. To a man in moderate circumstances, it must needs be a heavy blow.

(15) "I suppose it will make a great difference?" said Andy, inquiringly.

(16) "You can judge. Your father's property consists of this farm and three thousand dollars in government bonds. It will be necessary to sacrifice the bonds and place a mortgage of three thousand dollars on the farm."

(17) "How much is the farm worth?"

(18) "Not over six thousand dollars."

(19) "Then father's property is nearly all swept away."

(20) "Yes," said his mother, sadly. "Hereafter he will receive no help from outside interest, and will, besides, have to pay interest on a mortgage of three thousand dollars, at six per cent."

(21) "One hundred and eighty dollars."

(22) "Yes."

(23) "Altogether, then, it will diminish our income by rather more than three hundred dollars."

(24) "Yes, Andy."

(25) "That is about what my education has been costing father," said Andy, in a low voice.

(26) He began to see how this misfortune was going to affect him.

(27) "I am afraid," faltered Mrs. Grant, "that you will have to leave school."

(28) "Of course I must," said Andy, speaking with a cheerfulness which he did not feel. "And in place of going to college I must see how I can help father bear this burden."

(29) "It will be very hard upon you, Andy," said his mother, in a tone of sympathy.

(30) "I shall be sorry, of course, mother; but there are plenty of boys who don't go to college. I shall be no worse off than they."

(31) "I am glad you bear the disappointment so well, Andy. It is of you your father and I have thought chiefly since the blow fell upon us."

(32) "Who will advance father the money on mortgage, mother?"

(33) "Squire Carter has expressed a willingness to do so. He will be here this evening to talk it over."

(34) "I am sorry for that, mother. He is a hard man. If there is a chance to take advantage of father, he won't hesitate to do it."

13. As it used in paragraph 1, the phrase *different eyes* means which of the following?

a. Andy's eyes have changed color
b. Andy now wears glasses
c. Andy sees that the mood in the house has changed
d. Andy is happy to be home

14. Read this sentence from paragraph 14:

To a man in moderate circumstances, it must needs be a heavy blow.

The author uses the metaphor a *heavy blow* to indicate which of the following?

a. Andy's father is in a difficult situation
b. Andy won't be able to go back to school
c. Andy's father has lost over six thousand dollars
d. Andy is disappointed about his family's problems

15. Which of these is the best summary of the selection?

a. Andy Grant comes home from school and discovers that his father has won six thousand dollars. He will use the money to buy equipment for the farm. Andy finds out that he will need to leave school in order to help his father on the farm and work for Squire Carter
b. Andy Grant goes home and discovers that his family has fallen upon misfortune. Nathan Lawrence, the bank's cashier, has stolen twenty thousand dollars of Andy's father's money. Now that Andy's family has lost so much money, they won't be able to pay for his education and he'll have to leave school
c. Andy Grant's father has lost six thousand dollars because Nathan Lawrence stole it. This loss will cost Andy's family a lot of money. Since Andy's family pays $300 a month for his school, he will have to stop going to school. Andy is very cheerful that he doesn't have to go to school. He decides to work for Squire Carter in order to help his family
d. Andy Grant's family has suffered a misfortune because the bank's cashier stole money, some of which belonged to Andy's father. Without the money, Andy's family will have trouble paying its bills, including Andy's school bills. Andy will have to stop going to school. Furthermore, his father will have to borrow money

16. What phrase or sentence from the selection best shows Andy's feelings about having to leave school?

a. He began to see how this misfortune was going to affect him
b. Speaking with a cheerfulness which he did not feel
c. And in place of going to college I must see how I can help father bear this burden
d. I am sorry for that, mother

Questions 17 – 21 pertain to the following passage:

The Telegraph Boy by Horatio Alger

(1) Our hero found himself in a dirty apartment, provided with a bar, over which was a placard, inscribed:—

(2) "FREE LUNCH."

(3) "How much money have you got, Frank?" inquired Montagu Percy.

(4) "Twenty-five cents."

(5) "Lunch at this establishment is free," said Montagu; "but you are expected to order some drink. What will you have?"

(6) "I don't care for any drink except a glass of water."

(7) "All right; I will order for you, as the rules of the establishment require it; but I will drink your glass myself. Eat whatever you like."

(8) Frank took a sandwich from a plate on the counter and ate it with relish, for he was hungry. Meanwhile his companion emptied the two glasses, and ordered another.

(9) "Can you pay for these drinks?" asked the bar-tender, suspiciously.

(10) "Sir, I never order what I cannot pay for."

(11) "I don't know about that. You've been in here and taken lunch more than once without drinking anything."

(12) "It may be so. I will make up for it now. Another glass, please."

(13) "First pay for what you have already drunk."

(14) "Frank, hand me your money," said Montagu.

(15) Frank incautiously handed him his small stock of money, which he saw instantly transferred to the bar-tender.

(16) "That is right, I believe," said Montagu Percy.

(17) The bar-keeper nodded, and Percy, transferring his attention to the free lunch, stowed away a large amount.

(18) Frank observed with some uneasiness the transfer of his entire cash capital to the bartender; but concluded that Mr. Percy would refund a part after they went out. As they reached the street he broached the subject.

(19) "I didn't agree to pay for both dinners," he said, uneasily.

(20) "Of course not. It will be my treat next time. That will be fair, won't it?"

(21) "But I would rather you would give me back a part of my money. I may not see you again."

(22) "I will be in the Park to-morrow at one o'clock."

(23) "Give me back ten cents, then," said Frank, uneasily. "That was all the money I had."

(24) "I am really sorry, but I haven't a penny about me. I'll make it right to-morrow. Good-day, my young friend. Be virtuous and you will be happy."

(25) Frank looked after the shabby figure ruefully. He felt that he had been taken in and done for. His small capital had vanished, and he was adrift in the streets of a strange city without a penny.

17. Why did Frank give Mr. Percy all his money?

a. He was feeling generous
b. Mr. Percy offered to pay for the sandwiches
c. He owed it to Mr. Percy
d. He thought Mr. Percy would give him some of it back

18. What does the phrase "his small capital" mean in paragraph 25?

a. Frank's penny
b. Frank's twenty-five cents
c. Frank's virtuous nature
d. Frank's friendship with Mr. Percy

19. Why did Frank agree to eat lunch?

a. Mr. Percy was paying for it
b. Lunch was completely free
c. He only needed to buy a drink
d. He wanted to spend time with Mr. Percy

20. Is Mr. Percy likely to pay Frank back?

a. Yes, because he never orders what he cannot pay for
b. Yes, because he will be in the Park the next day at one o'clock
c. No, because Frank is not virtuous or happy
d. No, because he's shown that he does not have any money

21. What adjective best describes Frank's feelings in paragraph 25?

a. Disappointed
b. Incautious
c. Uneasy
d. Suspicious

Questions 22 – 25 pertain to both "Andy Grant's Pluck" and "The Telegraph Boy passages":

22. How are Andy and Frank similar?

a. They both have loving families
b. They both have experienced misfortune
c. They both were tricked
d. They both need money for food

23. How are "Andy Grant's Pluck" and "The Telegraph Boy" different?

a. "Andy Grant's Pluck" explains the circumstances that led to Andy's family misfortune, and "The Telegraph Boy" does not explain how Frank ended up with no money at all
b. Andy is all alone, but Frank has many friends who can help him
c. In "Andy Grant's Pluck," Andy is the victim of his family's bad luck but Frank in "The Telegraph Boy" is in trouble because he lost his own money
d. "Andy Grant's Pluck" is about how Andy was tricked, and "The Telegraph Boy" is about how Frank lost his money

24. Both selections end with the main characters

a. Feeling hopeful about the future
b. Looking forward to going back to school
c. In a dangerous situation
d. Feeling uncertain about the future

25. Which of these sentences or phrases from "Andy Grant's Pluck" could also describe how Frank in the "The Telegraph Boy" feels at the end of the selection?

a. He will receive no help from outside interest
b. I must see how I can help father bear this burden
c. Speaking with a cheerfulness which he did not feel
d. We have met with misfortune

Questions 26 -31 pertain to the following passage:

***The Great Round World and What is Going On In It* by William Beverley Harison**

(1) There is a new cause for supposing that the Treaty with Great Britain will either be defeated in the Senate, or else delayed for some time to come.

(2) This new trouble concerns the building of the Nicaragua Canal.

(3) It seems a remote cause, does it not? but it only shows how closely the affairs of one nation are bound up with those of all the others. No matter what our speech, our climate, or our color, we are all a portion of the great human family, and the good of one is the good of all.

(4) The Nicaragua Canal is a water-way that will cross the narrow neck of land that makes Central America. It will connect the Atlantic Ocean with the Pacific Ocean.

(5) With the help of such a canal, ships in going to the western coast of North or South America will not need to make the long and dangerous voyage around Cape Horn.

(6) Cape Horn, you will see if you look on your map, is the extreme southerly point of South America.

(7) There are so many storms and fogs there, that the Horn, as it is called, is much dreaded by sailors.

(8) Since the invention of steam, all the steamships go through the Straits of Magellan, and save the passage round the Horn; but there is not enough wind for sailing vessels in the rocky and narrow straits, so they still have to take the outside passage.

(9) The Straits of Magellan divide the main continent of South America from a group of islands, called Tierra del Fuego, and Cape Horn is the most southerly point of this archipelago.

(10) The journey down the coast of South America on the east, and up again on the west, takes such a long time, that the desire for a canal across the narrow neck of land which joins North and South America has been in men's minds for many years.

(11) A railway was built across the Isthmus of Panama to shorten the distance, and save taking the passage round the Horn. Travellers left their ship at one side of the Isthmus, and took the train over to the other, where they went on board another ship, which would take them the rest of their journey.

(12) This plan greatly increased the expense of the journey, and the canal was still so much wanted, that at last the Panama Canal was begun.

(13) You have all heard about the Panama Canal, which was to do the same work that the Nicaragua Canal is to do, that is, to connect the Atlantic and Pacific Oceans. You have probably heard how much time, labor, and human life was wasted over it, and how much trouble its failure caused in France.

(14) This Canal was to cut across the Isthmus at its very narrowest point. It was worked on for years, every one believing that it would be opened to ships before very long. Many of the maps and geographies that were printed in the eighties said that the Panama Canal would be opened in 1888, or at latest in 1889.

(15) No one expected what afterward happened. In 1889 the works were stopped for want of money; the affairs of the Canal were looked into; it was found that there had been dishonesty and fraud, and in 1892 the great Count Ferdinand de Lesseps, who built the Suez Canal, and a number of other prominent Frenchmen, were arrested for dealing dishonestly with the money subscribed for the Canal.

(16) There was a dreadful scandal; many of the high French officials had to give up their positions, and run away for fear of arrest.

(17) When the whole matter was understood, it was found that, for months before the work was stopped, the men who had charge of the Canal had decided that the work would cost such an enormous sum of money that it would be almost an impossibility to complete it.

(18) They did not have the honesty to let this be known, but allowed people to go on subscribing money, a part of which they put in their own pockets, and spent the rest in bribing the French newspapers not to tell the truth about the Canal.

(19) The worst of it was, that the money which had been subscribed was not from rich people, who would feel its loss very little, but from poor people, who put their savings, and

the money they were storing away for their old age, into the Canal; and when they lost it, it meant misery and poverty to them.

(20) So the Panama Canal failed.

(21) But the project of making a canal was not given up. Two years before the idea of digging at Panama had been thought of, the ground where the Nicaragua Canal is being built had been surveyed, and thought better suited to the purpose than Panama.

(22) The reason for this was, that at Panama a long and deep cut had to be made through the mountains. This had to be done by blasting, in much the same way that the rocks are cleared away to build houses. This is a long and tedious work.

(23) The Nicaragua Canal will be 159 miles long, while the Panama, if it is ever completed, will be only 59 miles; but of these 159 miles, 117 are through the Nicaragua Lake and the San Juan River—water-ways already made by nature. For the remaining distance, there are other river-beds that will be used, and only 21 miles will actually have to be cut through.

(24) The main objection to this route for the Canal is, that there is a volcano on an island in the Nicaragua Lake, and there are always fears of eruptions and earthquakes in the neighborhood of volcanoes. A great eruption of the volcano might change the course of a river, or alter the face of the country so much, that the Canal might have to be largely remade.

26. The author mentions the treaty with Great Britain in paragraph 1 because people are concerned about

a. A canal through Cape Horn
b. The new Panama Canal
c. The building of the Nicaragua Canal
d. The Central America Canal

27. What are paragraphs 15-19 mostly about?

a. The building of the Suez Canal
b. The financial problems that ended the Panama Canal project
c. The French newspapers, which did not tell the truth about the canal
d. Ferdinand de Lesseps' experience in jail

28. Which sentence best shows the purpose for building the Nicaragua Canal?

a. The new trouble concerns the building of the Nicaragua Canal
b. Cape Horn, you will see if you look on your map, is the extreme southerly point of South America
c. There are so many storms and fogs there, that the Horn, as it is called, is much dreaded by sailors
d. Since the invention of steam, all the steamships go through the Straits of Magellan

29. What is the tone of this passage?

a. Informational
b. Humorous
c. Mysterious
d. Angry

30. Why will the Nicaragua Canal be easier to build than the Panama Canal?

a. It is 100 miles longer than the Panama Canal
b. It needs to be blasted through the mountains
c. The San Juan River is already a complete canal
d. Most of the canal will go through existing waterways

31. Look at the time line below.

Canals Around the World

According to the passage, what is the correct order of the time line?

a. No change
b. 1, 3, 2
c. 2, 1, 3
d. 3, 1, 2

32. The author probably wrote this selection to

a. Argue against the building of the Nicaragua Canal
b. Argue for the building of the Nicaragua Canal
c. Explain the problems that ended the Panama Canal project
d. Discuss new plans for a canal

33. Which words in paragraph 22 help the reader know what *blasting* means?

a. Long and deep cut
b. Had to be made
c. To build houses
d. Long and tedious work

34. What is the main problem in building the Nicaragua Canal?

a. Many of the financial backers, like Ferdinand de Lesseps, are in jail
b. The route needs to be cut through mountains
c. The Nicaragua Canal is interrupting the treaty with Great Britain
d. The canal route goes past a volcano

35. Why does the author discuss the Panama Canal?

a. He is highlighting the other great canal in Central America
b. He is explaining the reasons why a canal is needed
c. He is showing the first canal that was attempted and why it failed
d. He is explaining how sailors avoid going around Cape Horn

36. Read this phrase from paragraph 19: *And when they lost it, it meant misery and poverty to them.* The author uses this sentence to show:

a. The people who suffered the most from the failure to build the Panama Canal
b. Why the Panama Canal failed
c. Rich people suffered the most from the failure to build the Panama Canal
d. The project of making a canal was not given up

37. The Nicaragua Canal will?

a. Make sailing longer and more dangerous
b. Help ships avoid Cape Horn
c. Cause more people to take the train across the Isthmus of Panama
d. Cut across the Isthmus at its very narrowest point

Questions 38 – 44 pertain to the following passages:

"The Ettrick Shepherd" by James Baldwin

Part I

(1) In Scotland there once lived a poor shepherd whose name was James Hogg. His father and grandfather and great-grandfather had all been shepherds.

(2) It was his business to take care of the sheep which belonged to a rich landholder by the Ettrick Water. Sometimes he had several hundreds of lambs to look after. He drove these to the pastures on the hills and watched them day after day while they fed on the short green grass.

(3) He had a dog which he called Sirrah. This dog helped him watch the sheep. He would drive them from place to place as his master wished. Sometimes he would take care of the whole flock while the shepherd was resting or eating his dinner.

(4) One dark night James Hogg was on the hilltop with a flock of seven hundred lambs. Sirrah was with him. Suddenly a storm came up. There was thunder and lightning; the wind blew hard; the rain poured.

(5) The poor lambs were frightened. The shepherd and his dog could not keep them together. Some of them ran towards the east, some towards the west, and some towards the south.

(6) The shepherd soon lost sight of them in the darkness. With his lighted lantern in his hand, he went up and down the rough hills calling for his lambs.

(7) Two or three other shepherds joined him in the search. All night long they sought for the lambs.

(8) Morning came and still they sought. They looked, as they thought, in every place where the lambs might have taken shelter.

(9) At last James Hogg said, "It's of no use; all we can do is to go home and tell the master that we have lost his whole flock."

(10) They had walked a mile or two towards home, when they came to the edge of a narrow and deep ravine. They looked down, and at the bottom they saw some lambs huddled together among the rocks. And there was Sirrah standing guard over them and looking all around for help. "These must be the lambs that rushed off towards the south," said James Hogg.

(11) The men hurried down and soon saw that the flock was a large one.

(12) "I really believe they are all here," said one.

(13) They counted them and were surprised to find that not one lamb of the great flock of seven hundred was missing.

(14) How had Sirrah managed to get the three scattered divisions together? How had he managed to drive all the frightened little animals into this place of safety?

(15) Nobody could answer these questions. But there was no shepherd in

Scotland that could have done better than Sirrah did that night.

(16) Long afterward James Hogg said, "I never felt so grateful to any creature below the sun as I did to Sirrah that morning."

Part II

(17) When James Hogg was a boy, his parents were too poor to send him to school. By some means, however, he learned to read; and after that he loved nothing so much as a good book.

(18) There were no libraries near him, and it was hard for him to get books. But he was anxious to learn. Whenever he could buy or borrow a volume of prose or verse he carried it with him until he had read it through. While watching his flocks, he spent much of his time in reading. He loved poetry and soon began to write poems of his own. These poems were read and admired by many people.

(19) The name of James Hogg became known all over Scotland. He was often called the Ettrick Shepherd, because he was the keeper of sheep near the Ettrick Water.

(20) Many of his poems are still read and loved by children as well as by grown up men and women. Here is one:

A Boy's Song

Where the pools are bright and deep,
Where the gray trout lies asleep,
Up the river and o'er the lea,
That's the way for Billy and me.
Where the blackbird sings the latest,
Where the hawthorn blooms the sweetest,
Where the nestlings chirp and flee,
That's the way for Billy and me.
Where the mowers mow the cleanest,
Where the hay lies thick and greenest,

There to trace the homeward bee,
That's the way for Billy and me.
Where the hazel bank is steepest,
Where the shadow falls the deepest,
Where the clustering nuts fall free,
That's the way for Billy and me.
Why the boys should drive away,
Little maidens from their play,
Or love to banter and fight so well,
That's the thing I never could tell.
But this I know, I love to play
In the meadow, among the hay—
Up the water, and o'er the lea,
That's the way for Billy and me.

38. Why is James Hogg called the Ettrick Shepherd?

a. He lived in Scotland
b. He kept sheep
c. He lived near Ettrick Water
d. He lived near Ettrick Water and kept sheep

39. Which of the following best describes the problem in paragraphs 1-16?

a. The sheep ran away and James Hogg couldn't find them
b. A storm came up and Sirrah got scared
c. James Hogg had trouble of taking care of such a large flock
d. James Hogg got lost in the darkness

40. What does the phrase, *Where the blackbird sings the latest*, from the poem "A Boy's Song" refer to?

a. James and Billy's favorite type of bird
b. A place where James and Billy like to play
c. The hay
d. James and Billy's favorite song

41. In paragraphs 11-16, how does James know all the sheep were in the ravine?

a. Sirrah told him
b. He counted the sheep
c. He rounded them all up from the east, the west, and the south
d. He was the best shepherd in Scotland

42. What does the poem show about the narrator's personality?

a. He is playful
b. He is afraid of shadows
c. He is not curious
d. He does not like to explore things

43. Use the story map to answer the question below.

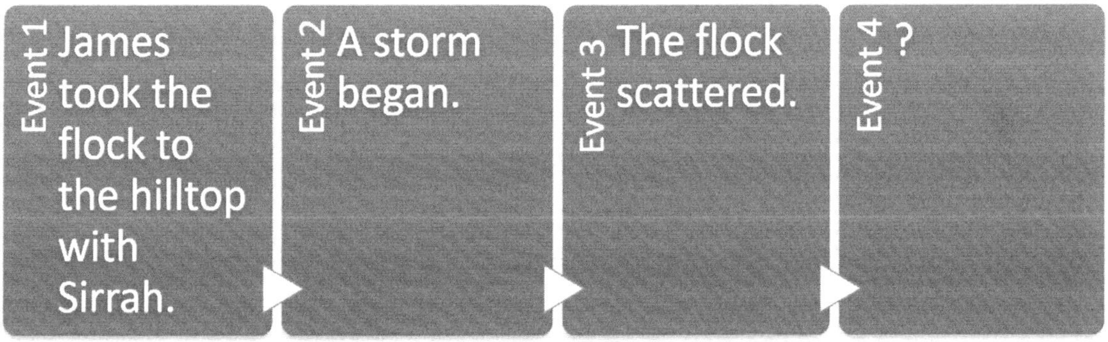

Which of these belongs in the empty box on the story map?

a. James wrote a poem about his sheep
b. James searched for the flock
c. James lived in Scotland
d. Sirrah gathered up all of the sheep

44. Why did James Hogg take care of the sheep?

a. He took care of them as a favor to the landholder
b. He loved the lambs
c. Taking care of the sheep was his job
d. He liked spending time with Sirrah

Answer Key and Explanations

1. C: The correct answer choice is C because paragraphs 2-5 introduce Buck and the setting in which he lives. The paragraphs accomplish this introduction by giving many detailed facts, such as the detail in paragraph 5 about the times he escorted Mollie and Alice on walks. Choice A is incorrect because two new characters, Manuel and the stranger, are introduced in paragraphs 7 and 8. While aspects of paragraphs 2-5 show Buck's personality, choice B is incorrect because the paragraphs also give other details about Buck, such as information about his parents and appearance. Choice D is incorrect because Toots and Ysabel are only mentioned in paragraphs 3 and 4. Furthermore, paragraph 4 says that he utterly ignored Toots and Ysabel, not that he is affectionate towards them.

2. B: The correct answer is choice B because the sentence indicates that Buck felt as if he owned or ruled over Judge Miller's place. The word *realm* indicates that the sentence is referring to everything. Choice A is incorrect because it talks about other dogs that came and went but does not show Buck's attitude towards them or Judge Miller's place. Choice C is incorrect because it shows Buck's opinion of himself but not his opinion of Judge Miller's place. Choice A is incorrect because it describes something that Buck enjoys, but does not give his attitude about the house and grounds at Judge Miller's.

3. B: The correct answer is choice B because details in the passage foreshadow what might happen to Buck. Phrases like "trouble was brewing" or "these men wanted dogs" indicate that one of the dogs men want or Buck might be heading for trouble. Choice A is incorrect because the paragraph does not give details about Buck's life; later paragraphs give those details. Choice C is incorrect because the paragraph does not give setting details. Setting details about Buck's current situation are given in later paragraphs. Choice D is incorrect because the paragraph does not describe any characters other than Buck; it does not indicate that Buck is the villain.

4. A: Choice A is the correct answer because the Klondike strike has caused people to look for dogs like Buck. Although paragraph 1 does not directly mention the Klondike strike, the reader can infer from paragraph 6 that the events discussed refer to the Klondike strike. Choice B is incorrect because paragraph 3 makes it clear that dogs came and went even before the Klondike strike. Choice C is incorrect because Elmo is Buck's father but not a main character in the story. Choice D is incorrect because the passage does not draw a connection between the Klondike strike and the frequency of the Raisin Growers' Association's meetings.

5. D: Choice D is correct because the sentence indicates that Buck considers himself to be like a king. Kings or royalty are often considered regal. Choice A is incorrect because nothing in the paragraph indicates that Buck is scared; in fact, Buck is like a king, which makes him unlikely to be scared of the other dogs. Choice B is incorrect because Buck doesn't indicate anger, which could be shown by barking or growling. Choice C is incorrect because *regal* is referring to Buck feeling like a king, which is unrelated to his happiness.

6. C: Choice C is correct because the first part of the passage mostly describes Buck's life, but the passage ends in a moment of change when the stranger wraps a piece of rope around Buck's neck. Choice A is incorrect because the passage does not describe a sequence of events as they happen. Instead the passage gives an overview of how Buck lived before the moment of change. Although part of the passage describes Buck's history, the passage also describes the moment in which his life changes, making choice B incorrect. Choice D is incorrect because the passage only describes life at Judge Miller's place but doesn't describe what came afterwards.

7. A: The correct answer is choice A because most of the passage provides background information about Buck's life and personality. Choice B is incorrect because the passage does not describe any moments in which Buck is acting heroic; instead, it describes Buck's regular interactions with the other people and animals at Judge Miller's place. Choice C is incorrect because the passage only briefly mentions the Klondike strike. The majority of the passage describes Buck's life. Choice D is incorrect because the other dogs are described in paragraphs 3 and 4. The rest of the passage focuses on Buck.

8. C: The correct answer is choice C because the stranger ties a rope around Buck's neck. This action indicates that Buck will be forced to leave Judge Miller's place. Choice A is incorrect because the end of the passage indicates that Buck might be forced to leave Judge Miller's place, which means he won't be able to continue to act like a king. Choice B is incorrect because the passage does not mention Buck or Shep at the end; Buck's parents are only mentioned in paragraph 5 when the passage describes Buck's family background. Although Manuel is a gardener, choice D is incorrect because Buck is likely leaving the garden to go away with the stranger, which means he won't be able to spend more time in the garden.

9. A: The best answer is choice A because the passage begins by setting up Buck's life and then showing a moment where his life is about to drastically change. Choice B is incorrect because only paragraph 5 refers to family; this is not a big enough portion of the passage to imply that the larger selection is about family. Although Buck might need to work hard in the future, choice C is incorrect because the passage does not have that many clues about upcoming hard work. Choice C is incorrect because the passage does not spend time showing that Buck strongly values relationships. The end of the passage indicates that Buck is about to experience a moment of change.

10. B: The best answer is choice B because paragraph 2 describes Judge Miller's place in great detail, including a description of the house, the driveway, the stables, and the outhouses. Choice A is incorrect because the paragraph only says that his place is in the Santa Clara Valley; however, the paragraph does not describe the valley in detail (it only describes it as sun-kissed). Choice C is incorrect because paragraphs 3 and 4 describe Buck's lifestyle, not paragraph 2. Choice D is incorrect because paragraph 2 does not mention the Klondike strike. The strike is referred to in paragraphs 1 and 6.

11. B: The correct answer is choice B because the sentence talks about how the men want dogs; the sentence foreshadows that Buck may be the type of dog that the men want. Choice A is incorrect because it refers to Buck's attitude around Judge Miller's place but does not hint at what might be coming next. Although part of the sentence indicates that Buck hopes to follow in Elmo's footsteps, the rest of the sentence simply describes Buck's father. Choice B better foreshadows what's going to happen in the story because it more closely relates to the events in paragraph 7 and 8. Choice D is incorrect because the sentence describes Buck's personality and interests without giving clues about what's going to happen next.

12. D: The best answer is choice D because, as a dog, Buck can't read. Although Buck may not be interested in current events, choice A is incorrect because choice D is a more logical answer. Choices B and C are also incorrect because the logic that Buck doesn't read the newspapers is drawn from the fact that dogs can't read.

13. C: The correct answer is C because Andy and his family were in good spirits, or happy, when he left for school at the beginning of the term. Now that he's returned, he knows something is wrong, but isn't sure what it is. Choice A is incorrect because the passage does not discuss Andy's eye color. The phrase *different eyes* is used metaphorically and does not literally mean that Andy has different eyes. For this reason, choice B is also incorrect. Choice D is incorrect because Andy is uneasy rather than happy. He knows something bad has happened.

14. A: Choice A is the correct answer because the phrase *a heavy blow* refers to the very difficult situation that Andy's father now finds himself in. The difficult situation hit him like a hammer, or heavy blow, because it was sudden and very financially painful. While it's true that Andy can't go back to school, choice B is incorrect because the sentence refers to Andy's father rather than Andy. Although losing six thousand dollars is part of the heavy blow, choice C is incorrect because the sentence does not show how much money Andy's father lost. The reader finds out the amount of money in paragraph 11, while the sentence in the question does not appear until paragraph 14. Choice D is incorrect because the sentence does not refer to Andy.

15. D: While parts of the other answer choices are correct, the best answer is choice D because it is the only choice that correctly summarizes the passage. Choice A is incorrect because Andy's father has not won six thousand dollars; he has lost that amount of money. Choice B is incorrect because Nathan Lawrence has stolen twenty thousand dollars, but only six thousand of that amount belonged to Andy's father. Choice C is incorrect because Andy is not cheerful that he doesn't have to go back to school; he likes school and is very disappointed.

16. B: The reader learns in paragraph 1 that Andy likes school. When Andy finds out he can't return to school, he is disappointed but he makes his voice sound cheerful when he's speaking to his family. Choice A is incorrect because it doesn't show Andy's feelings; it just shows that Andy knows how the family's misfortune will affect his studies. Choice C is incorrect because it simply contains Andy's new plans for the future and does not show his emotions. Choice D is incorrect even though this sentence does show Andy's emotions. However, this sentence refers to Andy's opinion about Squire Carter and not about returning to school.

17. D: Choice D is the correct answer. In paragraph 19, Frank says that he didn't agree to pay for both dinners, and then in paragraph 23 he asks for at least ten cents back. These two examples show that Frank thought Mr. Percy would return some of his money. Choice A is incorrect because Frank didn't intend to give all his money even though it may have been generous for Frank to buy Mr. Percy a drink. Choice B is incorrect because Mr. Percy didn't offer to pay for anything; in fact, he took money and didn't repay it. Choice C is incorrect because the passage does not indicate that Mr. Percy owes the money. Instead, it shows Mr. Percy tricking Frank in order to get Frank to buy him drinks.

18. B: The correct answer is choice B because the word *capital* refers to money. The reader can use the context of the passage to find the meaning of *capital*. Frank lost his twenty-five cents, which means his capital had vanished. Even though *capital* refers to money, choice A is incorrect because Frank had twenty-five cents rather than just a penny. Choice C is incorrect because Mr. Percy is the one who calls Frank virtuous. Choice D is incorrect because it's not clear if Frank had a friendship with Mr. Percy in the first place. Therefore, his friendship would not have vanished.

19. C: Frank knew he did not have much money, but when he saw that he would get a free lunch if he bought a drink, he was willing to eat it. Even though Mr. Percy handed the bartender the money, choice A is incorrect because Mr. Percy handed over Frank's money. Choice B is incorrect because lunch was not completely free; he needed to buy a drink in order to get the free sandwiches. Choice

D is incorrect because nothing in the passage indicates that Frank wanted to spend time with Mr. Percy. Instead, paragraph 8 says that Frank was hungry.

20. D: Choice D is the best answer because Mr. Percy used Frank's money in order to get the drinks. Even though Mr. Percy claims that he'll pay Frank tomorrow, the reader can infer that he is probably lying. Choice C is incorrect because Mr. Percy tells Frank to be virtuous and happy as a way of dismissing Frank. However, he does not withhold the money because he feels that Frank is undeserving. Choice A is incorrect because Mr. Percy ordered drinks that he could not pay for with his own money. Although Mr. Percy says he'll be in the park, choice B is incorrect because Mr. Percy might be lying.

21. A: Choice A is the correct answer because Frank has realized that he has just lost all his money. The word *ruefully* shows that Frank is disappointed. Choice B is incorrect because Frank acted incautiously earlier in the passage when he gave Mr. Percy all his money. By paragraph 25, Frank is no longer incautious. Choice C is incorrect because Frank feels uneasy in paragraph 23. By paragraph 25, Frank realizes that Mr. Percy has cheated him. Choice D is incorrect because Frank is no longer suspicious about Mr. Percy's actions; he already knows that Mr. Percy is not going to repay him.

22. B: The best answer is choice B because both Andy and Frank experience a form of misfortune. Andy's misfortune is that his family has lost money and he can't return to school. Frank's misfortune is that he is all alone in the city and does not have any money. Choice A is incorrect because only Andy has a loving family; paragraph 25 of *The Telegraph Boy* shows that Frank is all alone. Choice C is incorrect because only Frank was tricked. Andy's family lost money because a banker stole it from his father. Choice D is incorrect because only *The Telegraph Boy* shows that Frank experiences hunger. *Andy Grant's Pluck* does not indicate that Andy will have trouble buying food.

23. C: The correct answer is choice C because Andy has no control over his family's finances, while Frank's poor decision to trust Mr. Percy led to his misfortune. Although *The Telegraph Boy* does not explain how Frank ended up alone with only twenty-five cents, choice A is incorrect because *The Telegraph Boy* does show how he ended up with no money at all. Choice B is incorrect because Andy is not all alone (he has his family); similarly, Frank does not have many friends (he is all alone). Choice D is incorrect because Andy was not tricked; instead, his father was robbed.

24. D: The correct answer is D because both selections end after the main characters have suffered misfortune. They don't know what the future holds for them. Choice A is incorrect because the characters have only experienced bad things; they are not feeling hopeful. Choice B is incorrect because Andy in *Andy Grant's Pluck* can't afford to go back to school. Furthermore, Frank in *The Telegraph Boy* never mentions school. Choice C is incorrect because the characters are not in immediate danger; they are uncertain about their future, but there are no threatening things around them.

25. C: The correct answer is choice C because the sentence shows that Andy feels disappointed, or the opposite of cheerful. Frank also feels disappointed after he loses all his money. Choice A is incorrect because the sentence simply describes Andy's father's problem; it does not show feelings. Choice B is incorrect because it shows Andy's determination to help his father; *The Telegraph Boy* does not have any moments where Frank shows determination. Choice D is incorrect because it is stating a fact rather than a feeling.

26. C: The correct answer is C because paragraph 2 says, "This new trouble concerns the building of the Nicaragua Canal." Choice A is incorrect because paragraph 5 says that people are looking for a way to avoid going around Cape Horn; sailors would be happy for a canal. Choice B is incorrect because the Panama Canal is an older, failed project. Paragraph D is incorrect because there is no canal called the Central America Canal. There are two possible canals that, if completed, would cut across Central America: the Nicaragua Canal and the Panama Canal.

27. B: The correct answer choice is B because paragraphs 15-19 detail the many financial problems that hurt the Panama Canal project. These problems include the dishonesty of several people involved in building the canal. Even though paragraph 15 mentions the Suez Canal, choice A is incorrect because the paragraph only mentions the Suez Canal to explain who Ferdinand de Lesseps is. Paragraph 18 does mention the French newspapers, but choice C is incorrect because paragraphs 15-19 are mostly about the problems that hurt the Panama Canal. While the bribing of the newspapers was one of the problems, it wasn't the entire one. Choice D is incorrect because the paragraphs don't go into detail about Ferdinand de Lesseps' time in jail; they only mention that he went to jail.

28. C: The correct answer is C because the sentence shows the dangers of going around Cape Horn. Choice A is incorrect because the sentence only discusses the way in which the Nicaragua Canal is affecting the treaty with Great Britain. Choice B is incorrect because it only details the location of Cape Horn without explaining why this location could encourage people to build a canal. Choice D is incorrect because it discusses steamships without explaining why a canal is needed.

29. A: The correct answer is A, informational, because the author includes many factual details about the Nicaragua and Panama Canals. Choice B is incorrect because the author strictly gives facts and does not include jokes that would make the passage humorous. Choice C is incorrect because the author doesn't withhold details that would add mystery to the passive. Choice D is incorrect because the author does not show emotions such as anger; he has an objective tone.

30. D: The passage explains in paragraph 23 that the Nicaragua Canal will go through existing waterways, which means that the builders will not have to cut through much land. Choice A is incorrect because, even though the Nicaragua Canal is longer, only 21 of those miles need to be cut through. This number contrasts with the 59 miles of the Panama Canal that needed to be cut through. Choice B is incorrect because the Panama Canal needed to be cut through the mountains, not the Nicaragua Canal. Choice C is incorrect because the passage does not say that the San Juan River is a canal. It simply says in paragraph 23 that the Nicaragua Canal will go through the San Juan River.

31. B: Although the passage does not give the date of the building of the Suez Canal, it does imply in paragraph 15 that the Suez Canal was built before the Panama and Nicaragua Canals when it says "the great Count Ferdinand de Lesseps, who built the Suez Canal." The passage also indicates that the Panama Canal was attempted before the Nicaragua Canal; the reason the Nicaragua Canal needed to be built was because the Panama Canal failed. Choices A, C, and D are incorrect because they do not show the correct chronological order.

32. D: The correct answer is D because the author is discussing the new plans for a canal, which will be the Nicaragua Canal. The author does this by giving some background of canals in Central America and describing details of the Nicaragua Canal. Choices A and B are incorrect because the author is very objective and does not argue for or against the Nicaragua Canal project; instead, he just gives information. Although the author does explain the problems that ended the Panama Canal project (in paragraph 15-20), this description is a small portion of the passage. The main purpose is to describe the issues surrounding the Nicaragua Canal.

33. A: The correct answer is A because blasting will create a long and deep cut in the in the earth. The first sentence of paragraph 22 says that a long and deep cut needed to be made. The next sentence says that this cut will be made by blasting. Choice B is incorrect because the phrase 'had to be made' doesn't give details about how blasting works. Choice C is incorrect because the phrase 'to build houses' talks about building something up rather than blasting something away. Choice D is incorrect because, while blasting may be long and tedious work, the phrase does not describe what blasting it is. It just describes the type of work that blasting is.

34. D: Choice D is the correct answer because paragraph 24 says that there is a volcano in Nicaragua Lake, which the canal will go through. Choice A is incorrect because Ferdinand de Lesseps and the other people in jail backed the Panama Canal, not the Nicaragua Canal. Choice B is incorrect because paragraph 22 shows that the Panama Canal, not the Nicaragua Canal, went through the mountains. Although paragraphs 1 and 2 say that the treaty may be defeated or delayed, this treaty is not a problem in building the canal. In contrast, the building of the canal affects the treaty.

35. C: The correct answer is C because the author wants to explain what happened in the past with the Panama Canal so readers can understand the history as well as possible problems with the Nicaragua Canal. Choice A is incorrect because the Panama Canal was never completed, which means it's not the other great canal in Central America. Choice B is incorrect because the author explains why the canal is needed in paragraphs 4-11. These paragraphs come before the discussion of the Panama Canal. Choice D is incorrect sailors still needed to go around Cape Horn because the Panama Canal was never completed. If the Nicaragua Canal is completed, the sailors will then be able to avoid Cape Horn.

36. A: The correct answer is A because the sentence discusses the people who, according to the passage, were not rich, but lost money on the Panama Canal. These people suffered the most because they fell into deeper poverty. Choice B is incorrect because the sentence shows who suffered but does not show the problems that caused the money loss. Choice C is incorrect because paragraph 19 says that people who were not rich are the people who lost the money. Choice D is incorrect because paragraph 20 says that the canal failed and that the project was not completed.

37. B: The correct answer is choice B because the passage explains that the only way for sailing vessels to get from the Atlantic Ocean to the Pacific Ocean is to go around Cape Horn. A canal will cut across Central America so that ships no longer need to go around Cape Horn. Choice A is incorrect because the canal will do the opposite by making sailing less dangerous. Choice C is incorrect because people needed to take the train before the canal was built. The train was the only way for people to go between shores while avoiding Cape Horn. Choice D is incorrect because the Panama Canal was planned to cut across at the narrowest point. The Nicaragua Canal would be 100 miles longer.

38. D: The correct answer is D because paragraph 19 says that he lived near Ettrick Water and that he was a keeper of sheep. Choice A is incorrect because he didn't get his nickname because he was Scottish; however, people all over Scotland knew who he was and called him the Ettrick Shepherd. Choices B and C are only partially correct. Both answers contributed to his nickname. Since choice D includes both, it is the best answer.

39. A: The passage says that the sheep scattered during the storm. James couldn't find them in the dark, although he did find them the next day. Choice B is incorrect because the passage does not say that Sirrah was scared; it says that the sheep were scared. Choice C is incorrect because paragraph 2 says that James sometimes watched several hundred sheep; he only had a problem with so many sheep when they became scared by the storm. Choice D is incorrect because the passage doesn't say that James got lost; instead, paragraph 6 says that he *lost sight* of the sheep. He knew where he was, but couldn't find the sheep.

40. B: The best answer is choice B because the poem describes several of the narrator's favorite places. The key word from the phrase is 'where'. The phrase is describing a specific place. Choice A is incorrect because the poem does not indicate that the narrator and Billy prefer blackbirds to other birds. Choice C is incorrect because the phrase "Where the blackbird sings the latest" is referring to the meadow. The next verse discusses the hay. Choice D is incorrect because the narrator doesn't say that the blackbird's song is his favorite song; he just mentions the song.

41. B: Choice B is correct because paragraph 13 says that James and the other shepherds counted the sheep to determine that they were all there. Choice A is incorrect because Sirrah is a dog and cannot speak. Choice C is incorrect because Sirrah rounded up the sheep, not James. Choice D is incorrect because the passage does not say he was the best shepherd; in fact, the passage does not describe the quality of his skills at all.

42. A: The correct answer is A because the poem shows a sense of wonder and excitement. The last verse also says, "I love to play", which shows how much the narrator likes to play and have fun. Choice B is incorrect because the narrator does not show fear. Instead, he shows an enthusiasm for life. Choice C is incorrect because the poem shows a lot of curiosity; the narrator describes all his favorite places and may be curious about them. Choice D is incorrect because the narrator demonstrates his love of exploring when he describes all the details of the meadow, the hay, the water, and the lea.

43. B: The correct answer is B because paragraph 6 says that James started searching for the sheep once he realized they were gone. Choice A is incorrect because the selection does not indicate that James wrote a poem immediately after losing the sheep. Furthermore, the poem in the passage is not about the sheep. Choice C is incorrect because James always lived in Scotland; the answer choice is not an event that happened after he lost the sheep. While it's true that Sirrah gathered up the sheep, choice D is incorrect because it happened after James searched for the sheep.

44. C: The correct answer is choice C because paragraph 2 says that it was his business to take care of the sheep, which means that it was his job. Choice A is incorrect because the passage shows that being a shepherd is his business. He makes money from doing it, which means he's not doing a favor. Choice B is incorrect for the same reason; James may like the sheep, but he takes care of them to earn money. Choice D is also incorrect; while James liked Sirrah and says in paragraph 16 that he is grateful to him, James is a shepherd because it's his family's business.

Reading Practice Test #2

Questions 1 – 12 pertain to the following passage:

"The Cruel Crane Outwitted" from Indian Fairy Tales

(1) Long ago the Bodisat was born to a forest life as the Genius of a tree standing near a certain lotus pond.

(2) Now at that time the water used to run short at the dry season in a certain pond, not over large, in which there were a good many fish. And a crane thought on seeing the fish.

(3) "I must outwit these fish somehow or other and make a prey of them."

(4) And he went and sat down at the edge of the water, thinking how he should do it.

(5) When the fish saw him, they asked him, "What are you sitting there for, lost in thought?"

(6) "I am sitting thinking about you," said he.

(7) "Oh, sir! what are you thinking about us?" said they.

(8) "Why," he replied; "there is very little water in this pond, and but little for you to eat; and the heat is so great! So I was thinking, 'What in the world will these fish do now?'"

(9) "Yes, indeed, sir! what *are* we to do?" said they.

(10) "If you will only do as I bid you, I will take you in my beak to a fine large pond, covered with all the kinds of lotuses, and put you into it," answered the crane.

(11) "That a crane should take thought for the fishes is a thing unheard of, sir, since the world began. It's eating us, one after the other, that you're aiming at."

(12) "Not I! So long as you trust me, I won't eat you. But if you don't believe me that there is such a pond, send one of you with me to go and see it."

(13) Then they trusted him, and handed over to him one of their number—a big fellow, blind of one eye, whom they thought sharp enough in any emergency, afloat or ashore.

(14) Him the crane took with him, let him go in the pond, showed him the whole of it, brought him back, and let him go again close to the other fish. And he told them all the glories of the pond.

(15) And when they heard what he said, they exclaimed, "All right, sir! You may take us with you."

(16) Then the crane took the old purblind fish first to the bank of the other pond, and alighted in a Varana-tree growing on the bank there. But he threw it into a fork of the tree, struck it with his beak, and killed it; and then ate its flesh, and threw its bones away at the foot of the tree. Then he went back and called out:

(17) "I've thrown that fish in; let another one come."

(18) And in that manner he took all the fish, one by one, and ate them, till he came back and found no more!

(19) But there was still a crab left behind there; and the crane thought he would eat him too, and called out:

(20) "I say, good crab, I've taken all the fish away, and put them into a fine large pond. Come along. I'll take you too!"

(21) "But how will you take hold of me to carry me along?"

(22) "I'll bite hold of you with my beak."

(23) "You'll let me fall if you carry me like that. I won't go with you!"

(24) "Don't be afraid! I'll hold you quite tight all the way."

(25) Then said the crab to himself, "If this fellow once got hold of fish, he would never let them go in a pond! Now if he should really put me into the pond, it would be capital; but if he doesn't—then I'll cut his throat, and kill him!" So he said to him:

(26) "Look here, friend, you won't be able to hold me tight enough; but we crabs have a famous grip. If you let me catch hold of you round the neck with my claws, I shall be glad to go with you."

(27) And the other did not see that he was trying to outwit him, and agreed. So the crab caught hold of his neck with his claws as securely as with a pair of blacksmith's pincers, and called out, "Off with you, now!"

(28) And the crane took him and showed him the pond, and then turned off towards the Varana-tree.

(29) "Uncle!" cried the crab, "the pond lies that way, but you are taking me this way!"

(30) "Oh, that's it, is it?" answered the crane. "Your dear little uncle, your very sweet nephew, you call me! You mean me to understand, I suppose, that I am your slave, who has to lift you up and carry you about with him! Now cast your eye upon the heap of fish-bones lying at the root of yonder Varana-tree. Just as I have eaten those fish, every one of them, just so I will devour you as well!"

(31) "Ah! those fishes got eaten through their own stupidity," answered the crab; "but I'm not going to let you eat *me*. On the contrary, is it *you* that I am going to destroy. For you in your folly have not seen that I was outwitting you. If we die, we die both together; for I will cut off this head of yours, and cast it to the ground!" And so saying, he gave the crane's neck a grip with his claws, as with a vice.

(32) Then gasping, and with tears trickling from his eyes, and trembling with the fear of death, the crane beseeched him, saying, "O my Lord! Indeed I did not intend to eat you. Grant me my life!"

(33) "Well, well! step down into the pond, and put me in there."

(34) And he turned round and stepped down into the pond, and placed the crab on the mud at its edge. But the crab cut through its neck as clean as one would cut a lotus-stalk with a hunting-knife, and then only entered the water!

(35) When the Genius who lived in the Varana-tree saw this strange affair, he made the wood resound with his plaudits, uttering in a pleasant voice the verse:

(36) "The villain, though exceeding clever,

Shall prosper not by his villainy.

He may win indeed, sharp-witted in deceit,

But only as the Crane here from the Crab!"

1. In paragraph 26, why does the crab makes plans to defend himself?

a. He's worried that he'll fall
b. He's worried the crane won't really take him to the pond
c. He's friends with the crane
d. He's glad to go with the crane

2. Why are the fish skeptical of the crane?

a. The crane likes to help out fish
b. The crane is making the pond run dry
c. The crane likes to eat fish
d. They might fall out of the crane's beak

3. The context of paragraphs 13-16, helps the reader know that *purblind* most likely means:

a. Blind in one eye
b. Blind in two eyes
c. Old
d. Trustworthy

4. Why did the crane agree to bring the crab to the pond?

a. Because he always kept his word
b. Because the crab asked him to
c. Because the Genius told him to
d. Because the crab threatened him

5. The author organizes the story mainly by:

a. introducing Bodisat and showing his role in the crane's story
b. using cause and effect to show what happens when a pond runs dry
c. telling a story and then giving a moral
d. giving a moral and then telling a story that supports it

6. Which of these is the best summary of the selection?

a. The pond that the fish live in is drying up, and the crane offers to take the fish to a pond with more water. The fish don't trust the crane, so they send a representative to check out the new pond. He says that the pond exists, so they all agree to go with the crane. The crane drops them off at the pond and then comes back to take the crab. The crab also doesn't trust the crane, but the crane is honest and also takes him to the pond.
b. The pond that the fish live in is drying up, and the crane offers to take the fish to a pond with more water. The fish don't trust the crane, so they send a representative to check out the new pond. He says that the pond exists, so they all agree to go with the crane. Instead of taking the fish to the pond, the crane eats each one. He then goes back to the dry pond and offers to take the crab. The crab also doesn't trust the crane, but the crane is honest this time and takes him straight to the new pond.
c. The pond that the fish live in is drying up, and the crane offers to take the fish to a pond with more water. The fish don't trust the crane, so they send a representative to check out the new pond. He says that the pond exists, so they all agree to go with the crane. Instead of taking the fish to the pond, the crane eats each one. He then goes back to the dry pond and offers to take the crab. The crab also doesn't trust the crane, so he creates a plan to force the crane to take him to the pond. Just when the crane is about to eat the crab, the crab attacks him. The crane quickly eats him up.
d. The pond that the fish live in is drying up, and the crane offers to take the fish to a pond with more water. The fish don't trust the crane, so they send a representative to check out the new pond. He says that the pond exists, so they all agree to go with the crane. Instead of taking the fish to the pond, the crane eats each one. He then goes back to the dry pond and offers to take the crab. The crab also doesn't trust the crane, so he creates a plan to force the crane to take him to the pond. When the crane tries to veer away from the pond to eat the crab, the crab attacks him. The crane agrees to take the crab to the pond. When they get to the pond, the crab attacks the crane again.

7. The author mentions Bodisat at the beginning and end of the story in order to show that

a. Bodisat is the main character of the story
b. the story is non-fiction
c. the story is a fable
d. the story is realistic fiction

8. In paragraph 6, what does the crane mean when he says, "I am sitting thinking about you."?

a. That he's worried about the fish
b. That he's worried about the crab
c. That he's thinking of a way to trick the fish
d. That he's thinking about the larger pond

9. How are the crane and the crab similar?

a. They both live in water
b. They both like to eat fish
c. They are both deceitful
d. They both enjoy each other's company

10. In paragraph 30, what proof does the crane present?

a. The new pond is larger than the old pond
b. He ate the fish
c. He ate the crab
d. The fish are stupid

11. What is the moral of this story?

a. Villains succeed by being especially evil
b. Villains succeed by tricking others
c. Villains that are exceedingly clever are evil
d. Villains prosper by their villainy

12. In paragraph 27, what does the phrase "blacksmith's pincers" show about the crab?

a. That his claws close tightly
b. That his claws are sharp
c. That he wants to hurt the crane
d. That he's excited to go to the pond

Questions 13 – 16 pertain to the following passage:

"Five Children and It" by E. Nesbit

(1) The house was three miles from the station, but, before the dusty hired hack had rattled along for five minutes, the children began to put their heads out of the carriage window and say, "Aren't we nearly there?" And every time they passed a house, which was not very often, they all said, "Oh, *is* this it?" But it never was, till they reached the very top of the hill, just past the chalk-quarry and before you come to the gravel-pit. And then there was a white house with a green garden and an orchard beyond, and mother said, "Here we are!"

(2) "How white the house is," said Robert.

(3) "And look at the roses," said Anthea.

(4) "And the plums," said Jane.

(5) "It is rather decent," Cyril admitted.

(6) The Baby said, "Wanty go walky;" and the hack stopped with a last rattle and jolt.

(7) Everyone got its legs kicked or its feet trodden on in the scramble to get out of the carriage that very minute, but no one seemed to mind. Mother, curiously enough, was in no hurry to get out; and even when she had come down slowly and by the step, and with no jump at all, she seemed to wish to see the boxes carried in, and even to pay the driver, instead of joining in that first glorious rush round the garden and orchard and the thorny, thistly, briery, brambly wilderness beyond the broken gate and the dry fountain at the side of the house. But the children were wiser, for once. It was not really a pretty house at all; it was quite ordinary, and mother thought it was rather inconvenient, and was quite annoyed at there being no shelves, to speak of, and hardly a cupboard in the place. Father used to say that the iron-work on the roof and coping was like an architect's nightmare. But the house was deep in the country, with no other house in sight, and the children had been in London for two years, without so much as once going to the seaside even for a day by an excursion

train, and so the White House seemed to them a sort of Fairy Palace set down in an Earthly Paradise. For London is like prison for children, especially if their relations are not rich.

13. Read the sentence from paragraph 7:

But the children were wiser for once.

What are the children wise about?

a. They know that the house is nicer than it looks
b. They know the house is less nice than it looked at first glance
c. They know that being at a house in the country will be better than being in London
d. They know that the broken-down house will convince Mother to take them back to London

14. What phrase from the passage best shows the children's emotions when they arrive at the house?

a. And then there was a white house with a green garden and an orchard beyond
b. How white the house is
c. Everyone got its legs kicked or its feet trodden on in the scramble to get out of the carriage
d. It was not really a pretty house

15. Which of these best describes the selection?

a. The children are moving into a new house in London after living in the country
b. The children are moving into a new house in the country after living in London
c. The children are moving to a house in a new country
d. The children are moving from a prison to a fairy palace

16. What's the most logical reason why Mother was not in a hurry to get out of the carriage?

a. She's unhappy to be moving into the new house
b. She's excited to see the new house
c. She does not want to explore with children
d. She needs to help the driver

Questions 17 -21 pertain to the following passage:

"The Railway Children" by E. Nesbit

(1) "Wake up, dears. We're there."

(2) They woke up, cold and melancholy, and stood shivering on the draughty platform while the baggage was taken out of the train. Then the engine, puffing and blowing, set to work again, and dragged the train away. The children watched the tail-lights of the guard's van disappear into the darkness.

(3) This was the first train the children saw on that railway which was in time to become so very dear to them. They did not guess then how they would grow to love the railway, and how soon it would become the centre of their new life, nor what wonders and changes it would bring to them. They only shivered and sneezed and hoped the walk to the new house would not be long. Peter's nose was colder than he ever remembered it to have been before. Roberta's hat was crooked, and the elastic seemed tighter than usual. Phyllis's shoe-laces had come undone.

(4) "Come," said Mother, "we've got to walk. There aren't any cabs here."

(5) The walk was dark and muddy. The children stumbled a little on the rough road, and once Phyllis absently fell into a puddle, and was picked up damp and unhappy. There were no gas-lamps on the road, and the road was uphill. The cart went at a foot's pace, and they followed the gritty crunch of its wheels. As their eyes got used to the darkness, they could see the mound of boxes swaying dimly in front of them.

(6) A long gate had to be opened for the cart to pass through, and after that the road seemed to go across fields—and now it went down hill. Presently a great dark lumpish thing showed over to the right.

(7) "There's the house," said Mother. "I wonder why she's shut the shutters."

(8) "Who's SHE?" asked Roberta.

(9) "The woman I engaged to clean the place, and put the furniture straight and get supper."

(10) There was a low wall, and trees inside.

(11) "That's the garden," said Mother.

(12 "It looks more like a dripping-pan full of black cabbages," said Peter.

(13) The cart went on along by the garden wall, and round to the back of the house, and here it clattered into a cobble-stoned yard and stopped at the back door.

(14) There was no light in any of the windows.

(15) Everyone hammered at the door, but no one came.

(16) The man who drove the cart said he expected Mrs.Viney had gone home.

(17) "You see your train was that late," said he.

(18) "But she's got the key," said Mother. "What are we to do?"

(19) "Oh, she'll have left that under the doorstep," said the cart man; "folks do hereabouts." He took the lantern off his cart and stooped.

(20) "Ay, here it is, right enough," he said.

(21) He unlocked the door and went in and set his lantern on the table.

(22) "Got e'er a candle?" said he.

(23) "I don't know where anything is." Mother spoke rather less cheerfully than usual.

(24) He struck a match. There was a candle on the table, and he lighted it. By its thin little glimmer the children saw a large bare kitchen with a stone floor. There were no curtains, no hearth-rug. The kitchen table from home stood in the middle of the room. The chairs were in one corner, and the pots, pans, brooms, and crockery in another. There was no fire, and the black grate showed cold, dead ashes.

(25) As the cart man turned to go out after he had brought in the boxes, there was a rustling, scampering sound that seemed to come from inside the walls of the house.

(26) "Oh, what's that?" cried the girls.

(27) "It's only the rats," said the cart man. And he went away and shut the door, and the sudden draught of it blew out the candle.

(28) "Oh, dear," said Phyllis, "I wish we hadn't come!" and she knocked a chair over.

(29) "ONLY the rats!" said Peter, in the dark.

17. Which of these is NOT a reason why the walk to the house was difficult?

a. The road was muddy
b. There was not any light along the road
c. The walk was long
d. The road was not smooth

18. In paragraph 15, why did no one come to the door?

a. Mrs. Viney was running an errand
b. The train was late
c. Mrs. Viney didn't hear the knocking
d. The door was unlocked

19. Which state below best reflects the impression made in paragraph 24?

a. The house is homey and cozy
b. The house is not homey or cozy
c. Mrs. Viney lit a fire to welcome the family
d. The house is missing furniture

20. What can the reader conclude about the passage?

a. The children are excited to arrive at the house
b. The children love the train and railroad
c. The family is friends with Mrs. Viney
d. The children are seeing the house for the first time

21. Which sentence or phrase from the passage best illustrates why the author chose the story's title?

a. The baggage was taken out of the train
b. Then the engine, puffing and blowing
c. The children watched the tail-lights of the guard's van disappear into the darkness
d. Which in time was to become so very dear to them

Questions 22 – 25 pertain to both passages from "Five Children and It" and "The Railway Children"

22. What do the children in "Five Children and It" have in common with the children in "The Railway Children"?

a. They are excited to move into their new house
b. They are moving to an unfamiliar location
c. They are disappointed when they see their new house
d. They are eager to explore the country

23. Which sentence or phrase from "Five Children and It" shows that the mothers in both stories felt the same about the new house?

a. The house was three miles from the station
b. Mother said, "Here we are!"
c. Mother, curiously enough, was in no hurry to get out
d. But the house was deep in the country

24. What's the difference in the way the children in the two stories perceive their new houses?

a. The children in "Five Children and It" feel like their new house is a prison, but the children in "The Railway Children" are excited to explore
b. The children in "Five Children and It" feel like their new house is a prison, and the children in "The Railway Children" think their new house is run down
c. The children in "Five Children and It" are disappointed that their new house seems run-down, but the children in "The Railway Children" think their new house is a wonderful as a fairy palace
d. The children in "Five Children and It" think their new house is wonderful even though it's run down, but the children in "The Railway Children" are not excited about moving into a rundown house

25. Both passages are the beginning of longer works. What do these beginnings have in common?

a. They place the characters in a new setting
b. They place the characters in an uncomfortable situation
c. They introduce the characters by describing their appearance and personality
d. They foreshadow that the children in both stories will argue with their parents

Questions 26 – 37 pertain to the following passage:

A Child's History of England by Charles Dickens

(1) If you look at a Map of the World, you will see, in the left-hand upper corner of the Eastern Hemisphere, two Islands lying in the sea. They are England and Scotland, and Ireland. England and Scotland form the greater part of these Islands. Ireland is the next in size. The little neighbouring islands, which are so small upon the Map as to be mere dots, are chiefly little bits of Scotland,—broken off, I dare say, in the course of a great length of time, by the power of the restless water.

(2) In the old days, a long, long while ago..., these Islands were in the same place, and the stormy sea roared round them, just as it roars now. But the sea was not alive, then, with great ships and brave sailors, sailing to and from all parts of the world. It was very lonely. The Islands lay solitary, in the great expanse of water. The foaming waves dashed against their cliffs, and the bleak winds blew over their forests; but the winds and waves brought no adventurers to land upon the Islands, and the savage Islanders knew nothing of the rest of the world, and the rest of the world knew nothing of them.

(3) It is supposed that the Phoenicians, who were an ancient people, famous for carrying on trade, came in ships to these Islands, and found that they produced tin and lead; both very useful things, as you know, and both produced to this very hour upon the sea-coast. The most celebrated tin mines in Cornwall are, still, close to the sea. One of them, which I have seen, is so close to it that it is hollowed out underneath the ocean; and the miners say, that

in stormy weather, when they are at work down in that deep place, they can hear the noise of the waves thundering above their heads. So, the Phœnicians, coasting about the Islands, would come, without much difficulty, to where the tin and lead were.

(4) The Phœnicians traded with the Islanders for these metals, and gave the Islanders some other useful things in exchange. The Islanders were, at first, poor savages, going almost naked, or only dressed in the rough skins of beasts, and staining their bodies, as other savages do, with coloured earths and the juices of plants. But the Phœnicians, sailing over to the opposite coasts of France and Belgium, and saying to the people there, 'We have been to those white cliffs across the water, which you can see in fine weather, and from that country, which is called Britain, we bring this tin and lead,' tempted some of the French and Belgians to come over also. These people settled themselves on the south coast of England, which is now called Kent; and, although they were a rough people too, they taught the savage Britons some useful arts, and improved that part of the Islands. It is probable that other people came over from Spain to Ireland, and settled there.

(5) Thus, by little and little, strangers became mixed with the Islanders, and the savage Britons grew into a wild, bold people; almost savage, still, especially in the interior of the country away from the sea where the foreign settlers seldom went; but hardy, brave, and strong.

(6) The whole country was covered with forests, and swamps. The greater part of it was very misty and cold. There were no roads, no bridges, no streets, no houses that you would think deserving of the name. A town was nothing but a collection of straw-covered huts, hidden in a thick wood, with a ditch all round, and a low wall, made of mud, or the trunks of trees placed one upon another. The people planted little or no corn, but lived upon the flesh of their flocks and cattle. They made no coins, but used metal rings for money. They were clever in basket-work, as savage people often are; and they could make a coarse kind of cloth, and some very bad earthenware. But in building fortresses they were much more clever.

(7) They made boats of basket-work, covered with the skins of animals, but seldom, if ever, ventured far from the shore. They made swords, of copper mixed with tin; but, these swords were of an awkward shape, and so soft that a heavy blow would bend one. They made light shields, short pointed daggers, and spears—which they jerked back after they had thrown them at an enemy, by a long strip of leather fastened to the stem. The butt-end was a rattle, to frighten an enemy's horse. The ancient Britons, being divided into as many as thirty or forty tribes, each commanded by its own little king, were constantly fighting with one another, as savage people usually do; and they always fought with these weapons.

26. According to the author, why did the ancient Britons frequently fight with each other?

a. They had many weapons
b. They disliked the Phoenicians
c. There were no roads or bridges
d. They were divided into many tribes

27. What is paragraph 2 mostly about?

a. The Map of the World
b. The two islands and what they looked like
c. The two islands and the people who lived there
d. The winds and waves that blew against the island

28. Which sentence or phrase best shows the impact the Phoenicians had on the ancient Britons?

a. The Phoenicians traded with the Islanders
b. But the Phoenicians, sailing over to the opposite coasts of France and Belgium
c. These people settled themselves on the south Coast of England
d. The savage Britons grew into a wild, bold people

29. The tone throughout the selection is

a. humorous
b. informative
c. angry
d. bored

30. Which sentence or phrase best expresses the isolation of the islands of England and Scotland and Ireland?

a. Which are so small upon the Map as to be mere dots
b. The Islands lay solitary, in the great expanse of water
c. They can hear the noise of the waves thundering above their heads
d. Thus, by little and little, strangers became mixed with the Islanders

31. This passage is part of a longer work. Where does this selection most likely fit into the longer work?

a. The beginning of the entire work
b. The middle of a chapter
c. The end of a chapter
d. The end of the entire work

32. Read this phrase from paragraph 7:

But seldom, if ever, ventured far from the shore.

Why does the author include this phrase?

a. To show the ways in which the people used boats
b. To highlight the irony of making boats
c. To show where the people used weapons
d. To explain why the people built fortresses

33. What most likely tempted the French and Belgians to come over to Britain?

a. The white cliffs of Britain
b. The fine weather
c. The tin and lead
d. Juices of plants

34. This passage is mostly likely to appear in a:

a. Newspaper
b. Travel book
c. Textbook
d. Novel

35. Look at the time line below:

1. The Phoenicians began trading with the ancient Britons → 2. French and Belgian people moved to England → 3. The Phoenicians discovered tin and lead on the coast

Which answer choice shows the correct order of events?

a. No change
b. 1, 3, 2
c. 2, 1 3
d. 3, 1, 2

36. Why does the author begin the passage by describing a map?

a. To explain the location of the islands
b. To show the roads that run through England, Scotland, and Ireland
c. To show how the little bits of Scotland broke away from the main island
d. To show the size of the islands in relation to France and Belgium

37. What sentence or phrase best describes the lands in the interior of the islands (the parts away from the coast)?

a. These people settled themselves on the south coast of England, which is now called Kent
b. Especially in the interior of the country away from the sea where the foreign settlers seldom went
c. The whole country was covered with forests and swamps.
d. The ancient Britons, being divided into as many as thirty or forty tribes, each commanded by its own king

Questions 38 – 44 pertain to the following passage:

Ten Boys from Dickens

"The Boy Musician"

By Kate Dickinson Sweetser

(1) Johannes Chrysostemus Wolfgangus Theophilus Mozart—what a burden to be put upon a baby's tiny shoulders!

(2) If there is any truth underlying the belief that a name can in some measure foreshadow a child's future, then surely Wolfgang Mozart, who was born in Salzburg in 1756, came honestly by his heritage of greatness, for when he was only a day old he received the five-part name, to which was later added his confirmation name of Sigismundus. But as soon as

he could choose for himself, the little son of Marianne and Leopold Mozart from his store of names, selected Wolfgang, to which he added Amadeus, by which combination he was always known, and the name is for ever linked with the memory of a great genius.

(3) Almost before he could talk plainly the little fellow showed himself to be a musical prodigy, and when he was scarcely three years old he would steal into the room where his father was giving a lesson on the harpsichord to Anna (or "Nannerl," as she was called), the sister five years older than himself, and while she was being taught, Wolfgang would listen and watch with breathless attention.

(4) One day when the lesson was over, he begged his father to teach him too, but Leopold Mozart only laughed as he answered, glancing down into the child's serious face looking so intently into his:

(5) "Wait, my little man, thou art but a baby yet. Wait awhile, my Wolferl!" and the disappointed little musician crept away, but as soon as Nannerl and his father had left the room, the tiny fellow crept back again, went to the harpsichord and standing on tiptoe, touched the keys with his chubby fingers stretched wide apart until he reached and played *a perfect chord*! Leopold Mozart was in another part of the house, but his sensitive ear caught the sound, and he rushed back to find his baby on tiptoe before the harpsichord, giving the first hint of his marvellous ability.

(6) At once the proud and excited father began to give him lessons, and always, too, from that day, whenever Nannerl had her lesson, Wolfgang perched on his father's knee, and listened with rapt absorption, and often when the lesson was over, he would repeat what she had played in exact imitation of her manner of playing.

(7) Leopold Mozart, who was himself a talented musician, saw with pride almost beyond expression, that both of his children inherited his musical ability, and soon felt that Wolfgang was a genius. When the boy was only four, his father, to test his powers, tried to teach him some minuets which to his perfect astonishment, Wolfgang played after him in a most extraordinary manner, not merely striking the notes correctly, but marking the rhythm with accurate expression, and to learn and play each minuet the little fellow required only half an hour.

(8) When he was five years old, one day his father entered the sitting-room of their home and found Wolfgang bending over a table, writing so busily that he did not hear his father enter, or see that he was standing beside him. Wolfgang's chubby little hand held the pen awkwardly, but held it with firm determination while it travelled back and forth across a large sheet of paper on which he was scribbling a strange collection of hieroglyphics, with here and there a huge blot, testifying to his haste and inexperience in the use of ink.

(9) What was he trying to do? His father's curiosity finally overcame him and he asked:

(10) "What are you doing, Wolfgang?" The curly head was raised with an impatient gesture.

(11) "I am composing a concerto for the harpsichord. I have nearly finished the first part."

(12) "Let me see it."

(13) "No, please, I have not yet finished."

(14) But even as he spoke, the eager father had taken up the paper and carried it over to where a friend stood, and they looked it over together, exchanging amused glances at the queer characters on it. Presently Leopold Mozart, after looking carefully at it, said:

(15) "Why it really seems to be composed by rule! But it is so difficult that no one could ever play it."

(16) "Oh, yes, they could, but it must be studied first," exclaimed little Wolfgang eagerly, and running to the harpsichord, he added:

(17) "See, this is the way it begins," and he was able to play enough of it, to show what his idea in writing it had been, and his father and the friend who had before exchanged glances of amusement, now looked at each other with wonder not untouched with awe.

38. Why does Leopold Mozart refuse to teach Wolfgang how to play the harpsichord at first?

a. He does not think Wolfgang has talent
b. Wolfgang has already shown he is a musical genius
c. He thinks Wolfgang is too young
d. He only wanted Anna to learn harpsichord

39. This passage describes real people from history. Which aspect of the passage is most likely made up by the author?

a. The names of Wolfgang and his family members
b. The dialogue between Wolfgang and Leopold
c. The age at which Wolfgang composed the concerto
d. The speed with which Wolfgang learned to play minuets

40. Which sentence or phrase from the passage best helps the reader infer that Wolferl is a nickname for Wolfgang?

a. Johannes Chrysostemus Wolfgangus Theophilus Mozart – what a burden to be put upon a baby's tiny shoulders!
b. But as soon as he could choose for himself, the little son of Marianne and Leopold Mozart from his store of names, selected Wolfgang, to which he added Amadeus
c. He would steal into the room where his father was giving a lesson on the harpsichord to Anna (or "Nannerl," as she was called), the sister five years older than himself
d. "Wait, my little man, thou art but a baby yet."

41. In paragraph 5, Leopold says he does not want to teach Wolfgang harpsichord yet. What makes him change his mind?

a. Anna asks him
b. Wolfgang asks him
c. Wolfgang plays a chord by himself
d. Wolfgang composes a concerto

42. In paragraph 8, the phrase "a strange collection of hieroglyphics" most likely refers to

a. letters in a foreign language
b. pictures and shapes
c. sentences and paragraphs
d. music notes

43. What is the most logical reason why Leopold wants Anna and Wolfgang to play the harpsichord?

a. He wants his children to work hard
b. He's also a musician
c. He wants to impress his friends
d. He knows Anna and Wolfgang love music and wants to please them

44. Look at the timeline below.

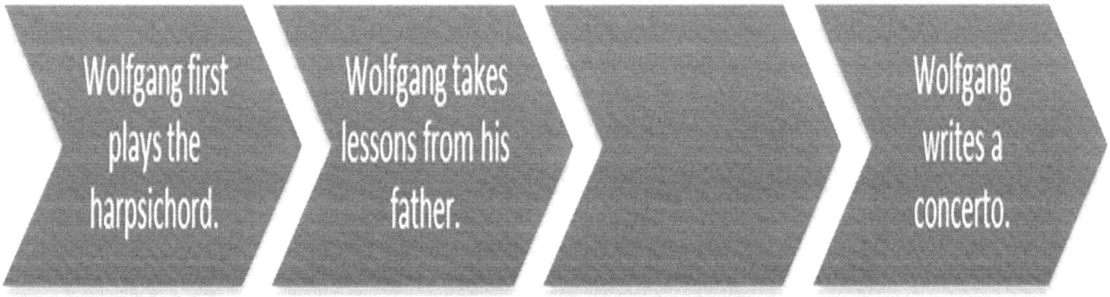

What event best fits in the missing arrow?

a. Wolfgang plays a perfect chord on the harpsichord
b. Wolfgang watches Anna's music lessons
c. Wolfgang amazes Leopold's friend
d. Wolfgang learns to play minuets in just a half hour

Answer Key and Explanations

1. B: The correct answer is B because the crab says in paragraph 24, "If this fellow once got hold of fish, he would never let them go in a pond." This sentence shows that the crab knows that he cannot trust the crane. Even though the crab says in paragraph 22 that he's worried he'll fall, he needs to defend himself from the crane because he's worried the crane will eat him. Choice C is incorrect because the crab is not friends with the crane; in fact, he does not trust the crane and is worried the crane will attack him. Although the crab is glad to leave the dry pond for the wet pond, he's worried about being transported on the crane because he knows that the crane will probably try to eat him.

2. C: In paragraph 11, the fish say that they think the crane is hoping to eat them, one after the other. They know that cranes like to eat fish and don't want to get eaten. Choice A is incorrect because skeptical means to not trust someone. If the crane liked helping the fish out, the fish would not be skeptical of him. Choice B is incorrect because the crane is not making the water run dry. Instead, paragraph 2 says that the water used to run short at the dry season. Choice D is incorrect because it is the crab that is worried he will fall, not the fish.

3. A: The correct answer is choice A because paragraph 13 says that the fish was blind in one eye. Choice B is incorrect because the fish is blind in one eye, not two. While the passage does say that the fish is old, choice C is incorrect because the word *purblind* contains the root word *blind* and is probably related to not being able to see. While the other fish do trust the purblind fish, purblind is most likely related to the word *blind*.

4. D: Choice D is the correct answer because the crab threatens to cut the crane's head off in paragraph 30. Choice A is incorrect because the crane demonstrates several times in the story that he does not keep his word. Choice B is incorrect because the crane intends to eat the crab instead of taking him to the pond. He only agrees to take the crab when he is threatened and does not care if the crab asks him. Choice C is incorrect because the Genius is a passive character that observes the crane's actions but does not interfere by giving him directions.

5. C: The correct answer is C because the author tells the story of the crane's trickery and then ends with a moral in verse. While the author does introduce Bodisat at the beginning of the story, Choice A is incorrect because Bodisat does not have a role in the crane's story; he only observes. Choice B is incorrect because the pond running dry is not the reason why the fish were eaten; the crane's trickery is the cause. Choice D is incorrect because the moral is at the end of the story, not the beginning.

6. D: While all of the answer choices contain correct parts of the story, only choice D is fully correct. Choice A is incorrect because the crane does not drop the fish off at the pond; he eats them instead. Choice B is incorrect because the crane does not take the crab straight to the pond. He tries to veer off to the tree to eat the crab and only goes to the pond when the crab threatens him. Choice C is incorrect because the crane does not eat the crab.

7. C: The correct answer is C because the mythical character of Bodisat and the moral at the end of the story show that the story is a fable. Choice A is incorrect because Bodisat is only mentioned at the beginning and end of the story; Bodisat observes the events but does not participate in them. Choice B is incorrect because the story does not display characteristics of non-fiction. For example, the animals speak, which cannot happen in a true story. Choice D is incorrect because realistic fiction portrays a made-up story that could happen in real life; since animals cannot talk in real life, the story cannot be realistic fiction.

8. C: The correct answer is C because the crane says in paragraph 3 that he wants to outwit the fish. Paragraph 5 says that the crane sat by the water and thought about how he should outwit the fish. Choice A is incorrect even though the crane pretends that he's worried about the fish. He pretends to worry about the fish so that he can convince them to go to the other pond. Therefore, he is lying in paragraph 8. Choice B is incorrect because the crane has not even met the crab in paragraph 6. Choice D is incorrect because the crane is lying in paragraph 10 when he talks about the large pond. He's really thinking about how he can trick the fish and find a way to eat them.

9. C: Choice C is the correct answer because both the crane and crab are deceitful, or tricky. The crane is deceitful when he tricks the fish and convinces them to let him take them to the pond. The crab is deceitful when he plans to attack the crane if the crane does not take him to the pond. Choice A is incorrect because only the crab lives in the water. The story does not say where the crane lives. Choice B is incorrect because the story does not say that the crab eats fish; in fact, the story doesn't say what the crab eats at all. Choice D is incorrect because the crane and crab are not friends. The crane wants to eat the crab.

10. B: The correct answer is B because the crane points out the fish bones underneath the Varana tree. Choice A is incorrect because the crane does not show proof that the pond is larger in paragraph 30; he shows the crab the pond in paragraph 27. Choice C is incorrect because the crane is talking to the crab in 27; he hasn't eaten the crab and can't show proof. Choice D is incorrect because the crab, not the crane, says that the fish are stupid.

11. B: The verse at the end of the story presents the moral and says villains won't prosper, or succeed, through villainy. Instead, villains win through deceit, or trickery. Choices A and D are incorrect because the moral says that villains don't succeed through villainy or evil. Choice C is incorrect because the moral does not say that clever villains are also evil. Instead, it says that the villain is clever.

12. A: The correct answer is A because the second sentence of paragraph 26 says that the crab caught hold of his neck securely, which also means tightly. Choice B is incorrect because no adjectives in the paragraph show that the claws are sharp; instead, the claws are tight and very secure. While the crab does have plans to hurt the crane, choice C is incorrect because the phrase "blacksmith's pincers" simply shows how tightly and securely the crab is holding onto the crane. Choice D is incorrect because the shape of his claws does not show the crab's emotions; his claws do not change shape based on how he's feeling.

13. C: The correct answer is C because paragraph 7 says that the children consider the house to be like a Fairy Palace even though it "was not a pretty house at all". The children are wise because they are glad to be living in the country, since London was "like prison for children". Choice A is incorrect because the paragraph makes clear that the house is run down and not pretty. Despite its looks, the children still love the house. Although the house is less nice than it appeared at first glance, choice B is incorrect because the sentence "But the children were wiser for once" means that the children knew that they would love the house despite its run-down appearance. Choice D is incorrect because the children do not want to go back to London. They are excited to be living in the country and considered London to be like a prison.

14. C: Choice C is the correct answer because the sentence shows the eagerness the children felt when they arrived. There was a scramble to get out of the carriage because the children were so excited to explore the new house. Choice A is incorrect because the sentence simply describes the house and doesn't hint at emotions. Choice B is incorrect because it only show's Robert's awe that the house is so white; it doesn't show how all the children feel. Choice D is incorrect because the children were excited to explore even though the house wasn't pretty; this choice doesn't show the children's excitement or other emotions.

15. B: The correct answer is B because the new house is in the country and paragraph 7 says that the children had been in London for two years. Choice A is incorrect because it is the opposite of what happened in the story. Instead of moving to London, the children are moving to the country. Choice C is incorrect because the children are not moving to a new country; they are moving to the country, which is an area that is not near a city. Choice D is incorrect because the passage uses *prison* and *fairy palace* as metaphors. The children aren't moving from a literal prison to a real fairy palace. Instead, they're moving from a city that felt like a prison to a house that feels like a fairy palace.

16. A: The correct answer is choice A because Mother does not seem happy to move into the house. She does not join in the "glorious rush" and thinks that the house is "rather inconvenient". Choice B is incorrect because Mother's hesitation to see the new house shows that she's not excited. While it's true that mother does not seem to want to explore with the children, choice C is not as logical a reason as choice A. The main reason why Mother doesn't want to explore the house is because she is reluctant to move in. Choice D is incorrect because the passage does not indicate that the driver needs help. Instead, Mother watches him carry the boxes in and pays him. She does this instead of exploring because she is not excited to move in.

17. C: The correct answer is choice C because the passage does not say that the walk was long. The passage does say in paragraph 6 that the family had to open and pass through a long gate, but it does not say that it was a long walk. All of the other answer choices are supported by the passage. The first sentence of paragraph five says the walk was muddy and dark. Paragraph 5 also says there were no gas lamps on the road. The second sentence of paragraph five says that the road was rough, which means it was not smooth.

18. B: Choice B is the correct answer because the cart driver says that the train was late in paragraph 17. Choice A is incorrect; the cart driver says in paragraph 16 that Mrs. Viney has gone home, not that she's run an errand. Choice C is incorrect because Mrs. Viney wasn't in the house. Choice D is incorrect because the door was locked; the cart man fetched the key from under the doorstep in order to unlock it.

19. B: The correct answer is B because the details about the house show that it's neither homey nor cozy. For example, paragraph 24 says that there is a stone floor, no curtains, no hearth rug, no fire, and rats in the walls. Choice A is incorrect because the house is the opposite of homey and cozy. Choice C is incorrect because Mrs. Viney did not light a fire for the family; paragraph 24 says that the fireplace had "cold, dead ashes". Choice D is incorrect because there is furniture in the house. Paragraph 24 describes the kitchen table and chairs.

20. D: The correct answer is choice D because the cart man shows them the way to the house and is the only one who knows where the key is. The reader also knows that the children haven't been in this town before because paragraph 3 says that the train was the very first one they saw on the railway tracks. Choice A is incorrect because the children don't show excitement. They are tired and cold. Peter's observation that the garden looks like "dripping-pan full of black cabbages" shows that he and his siblings are not enchanted by the house. Choice B is incorrect because paragraph 3 makes it clear that the children will learn to love the railway but don't love it yet. Choice C is incorrect because paragraphs 8 and 9 make it clear that the family does not know Mrs. Viney. Roberta asks who Mrs. Viney is and Mother explains that she hired Mrs. Viney to clean the house.

21. D: The best answer is choice D because the surrounding context shows that the phrase is talking about the railway. Since the story is called "The Railway Children", it is logical that the children might get this name because they love the railway. Although the other choices mention the train, they don't illustrate the reason why the author chose the title "The Railway Children" because they don't show the children's feelings about the railway. Choice A simply describes the action of removing the baggage from the train, choice B describes the train's engine, and choice C describes the children watching the train chug away.

22. B: The correct answer is choice B because both children are moving to a new house that they don't seem to know anything about. Choices A and C are incorrect because only the children in "Five Children and It" are excited when they see the house, and only the children in "The Railway Children" are disappointed. "Five Children and It" hints that the children are eager to explore the country in addition to the house, but choice D is also incorrect because the children in "The Railway Children" do not show this eagerness.

23. C: Choice C is the best answer because Mother in "Five Children and It" is not eager to see the new house and is not excited to move. Likewise, Mother in "The Railway Children" is also unhappy, as shown in paragraph 23 when she speaks "rather less cheerfully than usual". Choice A is incorrect because it states a fact rather than showing Mother's emotion. Choice B is incorrect because the words "Here we are" do not show Mother's state of mind; from these words, the reader cannot determine if mother is disappointed or excited to be at the house. Choice D is incorrect because it describes the house's location but doesn't show Mother's feelings.

24. D: Paragraph 7 in "Five Children and It" show that the children are very excited to explore their new house and are looking forward to living in the country. Many details from "The Railway Children" show that the children in that story are not excited about moving or their new house. For example, paragraph 2 says that they were melancholy and paragraph 12 describes the garden as a pan of black cabbages. Choices A and B are incorrect because the children in "Five Children and It" thought that living in London was like being in a prison; they don't feel the same way about their new house. Choice A is also incorrect because the children in "The Railway Children" are not excited to explore their new house; they seem reluctant to move. Choice C is incorrect because it's the children in "Five Children and It" that think the new house is wonderful. Likewise, the children in "The Railway Children" are the ones who are disappointed.

25. A: The correct answer is choice A because both families are moving to a new home in a new area, or setting. Choice B is incorrect because the children in "Five Children and It" don't seem uncomfortable; instead, they are very eager. Choice C is incorrect because the passages describe the houses in detail but don't focus on the characters. Although the children in "Five Children and It" don't feel the same way as Mother about the new house, nothing in the passages foreshadows an argument with the parents. The children seem to respect and get along with their mothers.

26. D: The correct answer is D because the author says in paragraph 7 that the ancient Britons were divided into many tribes, each of which had its own king. The author implies that these tribes fought among each other. While paragraph 7 also says the ancient Britons had many weapons, it doesn't say that the weapons were the reason that they fought. Instead, it simply says that they fought with the weapons. Choice B is incorrect because the text says the ancient Britons fought each other. It does not mention them fighting the Phoenicians. Choice C is incorrect because paragraph 6 says that there were no roads or bridges. The author gives this detail in order to describe the land. This detail does not support paragraph 7, which says the ancient Britons frequently fought.

27. B: The correct answer is B because paragraph 2 describes the natural details of the islands. For example, the paragraph describes the foaming waves, the cliffs, and the winds that blew over the forests. Choice A is incorrect because the map is discussed in paragraph 1, not paragraph 2. Choice C is incorrect because paragraph 2 only briefly mentions the people who lived on the islands. The author uses paragraphs 3-5 to give more details about the people who lived on the islands. Choice D is incorrect because the answer choice is only a portion of paragraph 2. The paragraph describes many natural features of the islands in addition to the winds and waves.

28. D: The correct answer is D because the word 'grew' shows that the ancient Britons changed after the Phoenicians arrived. Choice A is incorrect because the answer choice only shows something that the Phoenicians did with the Britons; however, it does not describe how the Britons changed. Choice B is incorrect because basket-work is something the ancient Britons did before the Phœnicians interacted with them. Choice C is incorrect because it refers to the French and Belgians who moved to the England; it does not mention the ancient Britons.

29. B: The author describes the history of the islands and gives informative details about the islands and the people who lived there in the past. Choice A is incorrect because the author does not make jokes during the article; instead, he simply describes facts. Choice C is incorrect because the author does not display anger or any other emotions; he simply describes facts. Choice D is incorrect because the author proves that he's very interested in the topic by giving many descriptive details. Therefore, he is the opposite of bored.

30. B: The word *solitary* refers to isolation, or being alone. Furthermore, the sentence says that the islands are alone in a great expanse of water, which shows that other lands do not surround the islands. Choice A is incorrect because the sentence only talks about the size of the small islands off Scotland. It does not talk about where the islands are in relation to other, bigger lands. Choice C is incorrect because it refers to people on the island, not the island in relation to the rest of the world. Choice D is incorrect because it shows the opposite of isolation; the sentence shows how the people who came to the islands (such as the French, Belgians, and Spanish) mixed with the ancient Britons.

31. A: The correct answer is choice A because paragraph 1 acts as an introductory passage. It starts by describing the islands on the map. Paragraph 2 moves into the earliest history of the islands. Later paragraphs describe the history as more and more groups of people came to them. Because of this organization, the passage best fits at the beginning of a longer work. The reader can infer that the author will continue describing the history of Britain throughout the rest of the work. Choices B, C, and D are incorrect because the first paragraphs of the passage are introductory.

32. B: The phrase "But seldom, if ever, ventured far from the shore" says that the boats didn't go far from shore. This implies that the boats may not have had much use in spite of the effort to build them. Choice A is incorrect because the text does not explain specifically how the boats were used. Even though the author describes weapons in the same paragraph, the phrase in the question focuses on the boats that the people made. The paragraph only moves onto weapons in the second sentence. Choice D is incorrect because the author does not connect the boats (discussed in paragraph 7) to the fortresses (discussed in at the end of paragraph 6).

33. C: Choice C is the best answer because paragraph 4 says that the tin and lead tempted some French and Belgian people to come over. Choice A is incorrect because 'white cliffs' are only mentioned by the Phoenicians when they are trying to explain to the French and Belgians where they have found the tin and lead. They point across the sea to the islands, using the white cliffs as a landmark. Choice B is incorrect because the fine weather was only mentioned as an example of when it is possible to see the cliffs. However, the weather was not mentioned as a way of convincing the French and Belgians to come over to the islands. Choice D is incorrect because the juices of plants were used by the islanders to paint their bodies.

34. C: The correct answer is C because the passage is informational and intended to teach children about the history of Britain. Choice A is incorrect because a newspaper is used to discuss current events and does not typically have long articles about history. While travel books sometimes have historical information, choice B is incorrect because the passage only talks about history. It does not describe the sites that travelers could expect to see. Choice D is incorrect because a novel is fictional, and this passage is non-fiction, or true.

35. D: The correct answer is choice D, as shown by paragraphs 3 and 4. The first sentence of paragraph 3 says that the Phoenicians found tin and lead on the islands. The first sentence of paragraph 4 says that the Phoenicians traded with the Islanders, who were also called the ancient Britons. Finally, the second-to-last sentence of paragraph 4 says that the French and Belgians settled in England. Choices A, B, and C are incorrect because they do not show the correct order that is described above.

36. A: Choice A is the best answer because paragraph 1 describes the location of the islands on the map. Readers know that they can find the islands by looking in the left-hand upper corner of the Eastern Hemisphere. Choice B is incorrect because paragraph six says that there were no roads that ran through England, Scotland, or Ireland during the time period that the passage is describing. Choice C is incorrect because the details about the small islands are only a small portion of the first paragraph. Most of the paragraph describes how the islands appear on the map. Choice D is incorrect because the paragraph does not mention the size of the main islands. Furthermore, the paragraph does not mention France or Belgium; these countries are first mentioned in paragraph 4.

37. C: Choice C is the correct answer because this answer choice describes the lands by mentioning swamps and forests. Choice A is incorrect because it does not give details of the lands and also does not mention the interior of the islands, which is first mentioned in paragraph 5. While choice B mentions the interior, it is incorrect because it only says that it is away from the sea. It does not give details about the lands. Choice D is incorrect because it discusses the dynamics of the tribes and the relationships between the people rather than the features of the lands, such as the swamps and forests.

38. C: The best answer is choice C because Leopold calls Wolfgang a baby in paragraph 5. He then tells Wolfgang to wait awhile, meaning that he will teach Wolfgang harpsichord when he is older. Choice A is incorrect because Leopold does not yet know that Wolfgang is talented. He only discovers that Wolfgang is talented after he plays the perfect chord in paragraph 5. Choice B is incorrect because Wolfgang first shows his talent in paragraph 5. Leopold does not realize that Wolfgang is a musical genius until paragraph 7, which is after Wolfgang has been taking lessons for some time. Choice D is incorrect because Leopold clearly implies in paragraph 5 that he plans on teaching Wolfgang harpsichord when he is older.

39. B: While it's possible that someone recorded the exact dialogue between Wolfgang and Leopold, it is more likely that the author invented it in order to tell a story. Since this scene took place in front of few witnesses who could remember the words and because there are no recording devices, it's unlikely that the exact words of the dialogue are true. Choice A is incorrect because the author should have been able to find the exact names of Wolfgang and his family members through historical research. Choice C is incorrect because it's logical that Wolfgang and his father might remember the exact age that Wolfgang wrote a concerto, which would be considered a huge accomplishment worth remembering. It is more likely that the dialogue is made up because the many words of dialogue would be more difficult to remember than Wolfgang's age. Choice D is incorrect because Leopold likely remembered how quickly Wolfgang learned due to his being very proud of him.

40. C: The correct answer is C because the sentence gives Anna's name and then gives her nickname, Nannerl, in parentheses. The nickname Nannerl is in the same form as Wolferl (-erl at the end). This detail helps the reader understand that Wolferl is Wolfgang's nickname. Choice A is incorrect because the sentence simply gives five of Wolfgang's names. Although one of the names is Wolfgangus, the reader doesn't yet know that Wolfgang's father is likely to abbreviate Wolfgang with the –erl ending. Although choice B also includes Wolfgang's name, it is incorrect because it does not show the types of nicknames used in Wolfgang's time. Choice D is incorrect because it does not give Wolfgang's name or explain how it is shortened into a nickname.

41. C: The correct answer is C because paragraph 5 shows that Wolfgang plays a chord by himself. The author emphasizes this feat by italicizing the words "perfect chord". Choice A is incorrect because Anna does not speak or ask anything at any point in the passage. Choice B is incorrect because Wolfgang does not *ask* his father to learn harpsichord. Instead, he comes into the lesson and shows his father that he wants to learn harpsichord by giving him a serious look (paragraph 4). Choice D is incorrect because Wolfgang composes the concerto in paragraphs 8-17, which is after he has already started taking harpsichord lessons.

42. D: Although hieroglyphics typically refers to letters in ancient Egyptian, they refer to music notes in this passage. It is clear that the 'hieroglyphics' refer to music notes in paragraph 11 when Wolfgang says that he is composing a concerto for the harpsichord. Choice A is incorrect because the word 'hieroglyphics' in paragraph 8 does not refer to the usual definition. While hieroglyphics are often made up of pictures and shapes, choice B is incorrect because they refer to the music notes used to compose the concerto. Choice C is incorrect because Wolfgang is composing or writing a concerto, not an essay.

43. B: Choice B is the best answer because the paragraph 7 says that Leopold was a talented musician. It also says that he was very proud that both of his children had musical talent. Although Leopold may have given Anna and Wolfgang a lot of work during music lessons, choice A is incorrect because it's not the most logical reason Leopold taught his children the harpsichord. If he simply wanted them to work hard, he could have engaged them in other activities. Choice C is incorrect because it is more logical that Leopold wants his children to excel in something that he also enjoys. Being able to impress his friends is an added bonus but not Leopold's main reason in teaching his children to play the harpsichord. Choice D is incorrect because nothing in the passage indicates that Leopold wants to please his children. Instead, paragraph 7 refers to Leopold's own musical abilities.

44. D: The passage describes Wolfgang's lessons in paragraph 6 and introduces the concerto in paragraph 8. The paragraph in between, paragraph 7, says that Wolfgang was able to learn minuets in under a half hour. Choice A is incorrect because Wolfgang played a perfect chord on the harpsichord the very first time he played the harpsichord, which happens in the first arrow. Choice B is incorrect because Wolfgang watches Anna's music lessons in paragraph 3, before he plays the harpsichord for the first time. Choice C is incorrect because Wolfgang amazes Leopold's friend in paragraph 17, after he writes the concerto.

How to Overcome Test Anxiety

Just the thought of taking a test is enough to make most people a little nervous. A test is an important event that can have a long-term impact on your future, so it's important to take it seriously and it's natural to feel anxious about performing well. But just because anxiety is normal, that doesn't mean that it's helpful in test taking, or that you should simply accept it as part of your life. Anxiety can have a variety of effects. These effects can be mild, like making you feel slightly nervous, or severe, like blocking your ability to focus or remember even a simple detail.

If you experience test anxiety—whether severe or mild—it's important to know how to beat it. To discover this, first you need to understand what causes test anxiety.

Causes of Test Anxiety

While we often think of anxiety as an uncontrollable emotional state, it can actually be caused by simple, practical things. One of the most common causes of test anxiety is that a person does not feel adequately prepared for their test. This feeling can be the result of many different issues such as poor study habits or lack of organization, but the most common culprit is time management. Starting to study too late, failing to organize your study time to cover all of the material, or being distracted while you study will mean that you're not well prepared for the test. This may lead to cramming the night before, which will cause you to be physically and mentally exhausted for the test. Poor time management also contributes to feelings of stress, fear, and hopelessness as you realize you are not well prepared but don't know what to do about it.

Other times, test anxiety is not related to your preparation for the test but comes from unresolved fear. This may be a past failure on a test, or poor performance on tests in general. It may come from comparing yourself to others who seem to be performing better or from the stress of living up to expectations. Anxiety may be driven by fears of the future—how failure on this test would affect your educational and career goals. These fears are often completely irrational, but they can still negatively impact your test performance.

Elements of Test Anxiety

As mentioned earlier, test anxiety is considered to be an emotional state, but it has physical and mental components as well. Sometimes you may not even realize that you are suffering from test anxiety until you notice the physical symptoms. These can include trembling hands, rapid heartbeat, sweating, nausea, and tense muscles. Extreme anxiety may lead to fainting or vomiting. Obviously, any of these symptoms can have a negative impact on testing. It is important to recognize them as soon as they begin to occur so that you can address the problem before it damages your performance.

The mental components of test anxiety include trouble focusing and inability to remember learned information. During a test, your mind is on high alert, which can help you recall information and stay focused for an extended period of time. However, anxiety interferes with your mind's natural processes, causing you to blank out, even on the questions you know well. The strain of testing during anxiety makes it difficult to stay focused, especially on a test that may take several hours. Extreme anxiety can take a huge mental toll, making it difficult not only to recall test information but even to understand the test questions or pull your thoughts together.

Effects of Test Anxiety

Test anxiety is like a disease—if left untreated, it will get progressively worse. Anxiety leads to poor performance, and this reinforces the feelings of fear and failure, which in turn lead to poor performances on subsequent tests. It can grow from a mild nervousness to a crippling condition. If allowed to progress, test anxiety can have a big impact on your schooling, and consequently on your future.

Test anxiety can spread to other parts of your life. Anxiety on tests can become anxiety in any stressful situation, and blanking on a test can turn into panicking in a job situation. But fortunately, you don't have to let anxiety rule your testing and determine your grades. There are a number of relatively simple steps you can take to move past anxiety and function normally on a test and in the rest of life.

Physical Steps for Beating Test Anxiety

While test anxiety is a serious problem, the good news is that it can be overcome. It doesn't have to control your ability to think and remember information. While it may take time, you can begin taking steps today to beat anxiety.

Just as your first hint that you may be struggling with anxiety comes from the physical symptoms, the first step to treating it is also physical. Rest is crucial for having a clear, strong mind. If you are tired, it is much easier to give in to anxiety. But if you establish good sleep habits, your body and mind will be ready to perform optimally, without the strain of exhaustion. Additionally, sleeping well helps you to retain information better, so you're more likely to recall the answers when you see the test questions.

Getting good sleep means more than going to bed on time. It's important to allow your brain time to relax. Take study breaks from time to time so it doesn't get overworked, and don't study right before bed. Take time to rest your mind before trying to rest your body, or you may find it difficult to fall asleep.

Along with sleep, other aspects of physical health are important in preparing for a test. Good nutrition is vital for good brain function. Sugary foods and drinks may give a burst of energy but this burst is followed by a crash, both physically and emotionally. Instead, fuel your body with protein and vitamin-rich foods.

Also, drink plenty of water. Dehydration can lead to headaches and exhaustion, especially if your brain is already under stress from the rigors of the test. Particularly if your test is a long one, drink water during the breaks. And if possible, take an energy-boosting snack to eat between sections.

Along with sleep and diet, a third important part of physical health is exercise. Maintaining a steady workout schedule is helpful, but even taking 5-minute study breaks to walk can help get your blood pumping faster and clear your head. Exercise also releases endorphins, which contribute to a positive feeling and can help combat test anxiety.

When you nurture your physical health, you are also contributing to your mental health. If your body is healthy, your mind is much more likely to be healthy as well. So take time to rest, nourish your body with healthy food and water, and get moving as much as possible. Taking these physical steps will make you stronger and more able to take the mental steps necessary to overcome test anxiety.

Mental Steps for Beating Test Anxiety

Working on the mental side of test anxiety can be more challenging, but as with the physical side, there are clear steps you can take to overcome it. As mentioned earlier, test anxiety often stems from lack of preparation, so the obvious solution is to prepare for the test. Effective studying may be the most important weapon you have for beating test anxiety, but you can and should employ several other mental tools to combat fear.

First, boost your confidence by reminding yourself of past success—tests or projects that you aced. If you're putting as much effort into preparing for this test as you did for those, there's no reason you should expect to fail here. Work hard to prepare; then trust your preparation.

Second, surround yourself with encouraging people. It can be helpful to find a study group, but be sure that the people you're around will encourage a positive attitude. If you spend time with others who are anxious or cynical, this will only contribute to your own anxiety. Look for others who are motivated to study hard from a desire to succeed, not from a fear of failure.

Third, reward yourself. A test is physically and mentally tiring, even without anxiety, and it can be helpful to have something to look forward to. Plan an activity following the test, regardless of the outcome, such as going to a movie or getting ice cream.

When you are taking the test, if you find yourself beginning to feel anxious, remind yourself that you know the material. Visualize successfully completing the test. Then take a few deep, relaxing breaths and return to it. Work through the questions carefully but with confidence, knowing that you are capable of succeeding.

Developing a healthy mental approach to test taking will also aid in other areas of life. Test anxiety affects more than just the actual test—it can be damaging to your mental health and even contribute to depression. It's important to beat test anxiety before it becomes a problem for more than testing.

Study Strategy

Being prepared for the test is necessary to combat anxiety, but what does being prepared look like? You may study for hours on end and still not feel prepared. What you need is a strategy for test prep. The next few pages outline our recommended steps to help you plan out and conquer the challenge of preparation.

Step 1: Scope Out the Test

Learn everything you can about the format (multiple choice, essay, etc.) and what will be on the test. Gather any study materials, course outlines, or sample exams that may be available. Not only will this help you to prepare, but knowing what to expect can help to alleviate test anxiety.

Step 2: Map Out the Material

Look through the textbook or study guide and make note of how many chapters or sections it has. Then divide these over the time you have. For example, if a book has 15 chapters and you have five days to study, you need to cover three chapters each day. Even better, if you have the time, leave an extra day at the end for overall review after you have gone through the material in depth.

If time is limited, you may need to prioritize the material. Look through it and make note of which sections you think you already have a good grasp on, and which need review. While you are studying, skim quickly through the familiar sections and take more time on the challenging parts.

Write out your plan so you don't get lost as you go. Having a written plan also helps you feel more in control of the study, so anxiety is less likely to arise from feeling overwhelmed at the amount to cover.

Step 3: Gather Your Tools

Decide what study method works best for you. Do you prefer to highlight in the book as you study and then go back over the highlighted portions? Or do you type out notes of the important information? Or is it helpful to make flashcards that you can carry with you? Assemble the pens, index cards, highlighters, post-it notes, and any other materials you may need so you won't be distracted by getting up to find things while you study.

If you're having a hard time retaining the information or organizing your notes, experiment with different methods. For example, try color-coding by subject with colored pens, highlighters, or post-it notes. If you learn better by hearing, try recording yourself reading your notes so you can listen while in the car, working out, or simply sitting at your desk. Ask a friend to quiz you from your flashcards, or try teaching someone the material to solidify it in your mind.

Step 4: Create Your Environment

It's important to avoid distractions while you study. This includes both the obvious distractions like visitors and the subtle distractions like an uncomfortable chair (or a too-comfortable couch that makes you want to fall asleep). Set up the best study environment possible: good lighting and a comfortable work area. If background music helps you focus, you may want to turn it on, but otherwise keep the room quiet. If you are using a computer to take notes, be sure you don't have any other windows open, especially applications like social media, games, or anything else that could distract you. Silence your phone and turn off notifications. Be sure to keep water close by so you stay hydrated while you study (but avoid unhealthy drinks and snacks).

Also, take into account the best time of day to study. Are you freshest first thing in the morning? Try to set aside some time then to work through the material. Is your mind clearer in the afternoon or evening? Schedule your study session then. Another method is to study at the same time of day that you will take the test, so that your brain gets used to working on the material at that time and will be ready to focus at test time.

Step 5: Study!

Once you have done all the study preparation, it's time to settle into the actual studying. Sit down, take a few moments to settle your mind so you can focus, and begin to follow your study plan. Don't give in to distractions or let yourself procrastinate. This is your time to prepare so you'll be ready to fearlessly approach the test. Make the most of the time and stay focused.

Of course, you don't want to burn out. If you study too long you may find that you're not retaining the information very well. Take regular study breaks. For example, taking five minutes out of every hour to walk briskly, breathing deeply and swinging your arms, can help your mind stay fresh.

As you get to the end of each chapter or section, it's a good idea to do a quick review. Remind yourself of what you learned and work on any difficult parts. When you feel that you've mastered the material, move on to the next part. At the end of your study session, briefly skim through your notes again.

But while review is helpful, cramming last minute is NOT. If at all possible, work ahead so that you won't need to fit all your study into the last day. Cramming overloads your brain with more information than it can process and retain, and your tired mind may struggle to recall even previously learned information when it is overwhelmed with last-minute study. Also, the urgent nature of cramming and the stress placed on your brain contribute to anxiety. You'll be more likely to go to the test feeling unprepared and having trouble thinking clearly.

So don't cram, and don't stay up late before the test, even just to review your notes at a leisurely pace. Your brain needs rest more than it needs to go over the information again. In fact, plan to finish your studies by noon or early afternoon the day before the test. Give your brain the rest of the day to relax or focus on other things, and get a good night's sleep. Then you will be fresh for the test and better able to recall what you've studied.

Step 6: Take a Practice Test

Many courses offer sample tests, either online or in the study materials. This is an excellent resource to check whether you have mastered the material, as well as to prepare for the test format and environment.

Check the test format ahead of time: the number of questions, the type (multiple choice, free response, etc.), and the time limit. Then create a plan for working through them. For example, if you have 30 minutes to take a 60-question test, your limit is 30 seconds per question. Spend less time on the questions you know well so that you can take more time on the difficult ones.

If you have time to take several practice tests, take the first one open book, with no time limit. Work through the questions at your own pace and make sure you fully understand them. Gradually work up to taking a test under test conditions: sit at a desk with all study materials put away and set a timer. Pace yourself to make sure you finish the test with time to spare and go back to check your answers if you have time.

After each test, check your answers. On the questions you missed, be sure you understand why you missed them. Did you misread the question (tests can use tricky wording)? Did you forget the information? Or was it something you hadn't learned? Go back and study any shaky areas that the practice tests reveal.

Taking these tests not only helps with your grade, but also aids in combating test anxiety. If you're already used to the test conditions, you're less likely to worry about it, and working through tests until you're scoring well gives you a confidence boost. Go through the practice tests until you feel comfortable, and then you can go into the test knowing that you're ready for it.

Test Tips

On test day, you should be confident, knowing that you've prepared well and are ready to answer the questions. But aside from preparation, there are several test day strategies you can employ to maximize your performance.

First, as stated before, get a good night's sleep the night before the test (and for several nights before that, if possible). Go into the test with a fresh, alert mind rather than staying up late to study.

Try not to change too much about your normal routine on the day of the test. It's important to eat a nutritious breakfast, but if you normally don't eat breakfast at all, consider eating just a protein bar. If you're a coffee drinker, go ahead and have your normal coffee. Just make sure you time it so that the caffeine doesn't wear off right in the middle of your test. Avoid sugary beverages, and drink enough water to stay hydrated but not so much that you need a restroom break 10 minutes into the test. If your test isn't first thing in the morning, consider going for a walk or doing a light workout before the test to get your blood flowing.

Allow yourself enough time to get ready, and leave for the test with plenty of time to spare so you won't have the anxiety of scrambling to arrive in time. Another reason to be early is to select a good seat. It's helpful to sit away from doors and windows, which can be distracting. Find a good seat, get out your supplies, and settle your mind before the test begins.

When the test begins, start by going over the instructions carefully, even if you already know what to expect. Make sure you avoid any careless mistakes by following the directions.

Then begin working through the questions, pacing yourself as you've practiced. If you're not sure on an answer, don't spend too much time on it, and don't let it shake your confidence. Either skip it and come back later, or eliminate as many wrong answers as possible and guess among the remaining ones. Don't dwell on these questions as you continue—put them out of your mind and focus on what lies ahead.

Be sure to read all of the answer choices, even if you're sure the first one is the right answer. Sometimes you'll find a better one if you keep reading. But don't second-guess yourself if you do immediately know the answer. Your gut instinct is usually right. Don't let test anxiety rob you of the information you know.

If you have time at the end of the test (and if the test format allows), go back and review your answers. Be cautious about changing any, since your first instinct tends to be correct, but make sure you didn't misread any of the questions or accidentally mark the wrong answer choice. Look over any you skipped and make an educated guess.

At the end, leave the test feeling confident. You've done your best, so don't waste time worrying about your performance or wishing you could change anything. Instead, celebrate the successful completion of this test. And finally, use this test to learn how to deal with anxiety even better next time.

Review Video: Test Anxiety
Visit mometrix.com/academy and enter code: 100340

Important Qualification

Not all anxiety is created equal. If your test anxiety is causing major issues in your life beyond the classroom or testing center, or if you are experiencing troubling physical symptoms related to your anxiety, it may be a sign of a serious physiological or psychological condition. If this sounds like your situation, we strongly encourage you to seek professional help.

Online Resources

Due to our efforts to try to keep this book to a manageable length, we've created a link that will give you access to all of your online resources:

mometrix.com/resources719/ssmcag8read

It's Your Moment, Let's Celebrate It!

Share your story @mometrixtestpreparation